ALONG
DIFFERENT
LINES

P.T.P

£1.00

ALONG DIFFERENT LINES

70 Real Life Railway Stories

GEOFF BODY & BILL PARKER

First published 2012

The History Press
The Mill, Brimscombe Port
Stroud, Gloucestershire, GL5 2QG
www.thehistorypress.co.uk

British Library Cataloguing in Publication Data.
A catalogue record for this book is available from the British Library.

ISBN 978 0 7524 8915 5

Typesetting and origination by The History Press
Printed in Great Britain

Contents

Introduction & Acknowledgements

The wide and most gratifying interest in our previous book, *Signal Box Coming Up, Sir!*, has led to this further collection of accounts reflecting the experiences of seasoned railwaymen in all branches of their industry. Their contributions have again showed just how varied and interesting the business of rail transport is.

Whatever the period, railways have always involved a wide range of activities: engineering, operation, commercial, financial, policing, human resources and so on. Some once quite sizeable activities such as grain sack hire and the carriage of livestock have gone, but the fundamentals of providing and managing movement remain in a business that is busier and more sophisticated than ever. Within this modern, streamlined railway the technical complexities – not always apparent – have increased, and the dimensions of higher speed and comfort, safety, environmental issues and cost-effectiveness have grown in importance.

To the basic infrastructure of the railway network at any period must be added the intricacies and challenges of its constant minute-by-minute operation, another factor adding to the incidence of the unusual, the admirable, the amusing and, sometimes, the unfortunate. Certainly much of the fascination of railways comes from their complex equipment and intense operation, but moving passengers and freight safely and efficiently, like everything else, depends on people. Thankfully, railways have, throughout their existence, been blessed with a superb and able workforce of men and women dedicated to those ends.

Our aim in this book has been to capture some of the most interesting examples of Britain's railway activity by asking a number of professional railwaymen to contribute recollections from their careers. Hopefully, if we have done our editing job well, this will result in an entertaining book filled with 'highlights'. The response we have had has been amazing, almost an embarrassment of riches, and we are extremely grateful to the contributors listed below. What they have written is, of course, based on their own views and memories, but for any shortcomings in the presentation we hold our hands up and apologise. The final product should not only entertain but emphasise the many personal qualities of the men and women who run the trains.

Thanks are due to other people who have encouraged or facilitated our efforts, including Colin Brown and especially Amy Rigg of The History Press and the staff there who combine efficiency with being nice to work with. We are also grateful to those who have supplied illustrations. Where not specifically acknowledged these are from the Geoff Body Collection.

Contributors: Philip Benham, Les Binns, Alex Bryce, David Crathorn, Jim Dorward, Colin Driver, Jim Gibbons, Hugh Gould, Tom Greaves, David Jagoe, Harry Knox, Mike Lamport, Don Love, the Hon. Sir William McAlpine, David Maidment, Frank Paterson, Graham Paterson, Bill Robinson, Dennis Simmonds, Alan Sourbut, Peter Spedding, Cedric Spiller, Theo Steel, Bryan Stone, Basil Tellwright, David Ward and Nick Wood.

Beginnings

Opening these accounts, Geoff Body remembers some of his early railway experiences. At the end, Sir William McAlpine portrays activities at the other end of the spectrum. In between is a range of fascinating stories from the professionals of a great industry.

My father was a district relief clerk and I was well used to train travel, especially from Peterborough to Waddington or Rauceby in Lincolnshire, the nearest stations to my respective grandparents. It became the practice for my parents to take a later holiday on their own after the annual family week at Sandown, Isle of Wight, in June, and when they did I went to stay on the farm of my Waddington grandparents. During one school holiday it was deemed that I, still a lad, was responsible enough to make the journey to Lincoln on my own. Suited me! I welcomed the opportunity and it saved my parents from having to deliver me before setting out on their own break. Put on the train at Peterborough I knew that I must get out at Grantham and move across the platform face to No. 4 bay where the Lincoln 'Parly' usually stood. I had to make sure this was the right train for sometimes the Nottingham stood there and sometimes the Lincoln one even went from the Up side bay.

Delivered onto the busy main-line train at Peterborough with plenty of admonitions about behaviour, I sat quietly all the way to Grantham, content to savour the travelling experience. Alighting at Grantham with my small suitcase and the demeaning label with my journey details attached to it, I checked on my next service and then devoted myself to the Nestlé chocolate machine and the views of the locomotive depot from the Down platform. Joining my own train, I was not displeased with my seasoned-traveller performance so far.

The Lincoln train was compartment stock with no corridor so I could travel in splendid isolation. I knew that I had to watch for Honington, Caythorpe, Leadenham, Navenby and Harmston station stops before alighting at Waddington. Plenty of time to switch the lights on and off, open the window and try the result with the strap on the various anchor points. I had enough sense to put my head out only with caution and gave that up for studying the stilted sepia photographs of unknown and uninspiring places displayed above each seat.

When these activities palled I settled down with my comic. Some cracking stories absorbed all my attention and I neglected to check the passing markers. Horrors! That was the brickyard on the Up side. I had missed Waddington station itself and was now heading for the unfamiliar territory of Lincoln Central, then a busy station indeed. I remember feeling highly embarrassed but not in the slightest bit worried. I just asked about the next train back and spent the waiting time marvelling at the

At Lincoln Central a good crowd of intending passengers awaits the approaching Colchester to York express headed by an English Electric Type 3 diesel. (Bryan Stone)

constant operation of the High Street level crossing and the variety of local trains waiting in the bays for various East Lincolnshire destinations.

There were no recriminations when I finally arrived. My grandparents with the pony and trap were waiting to take me to their farm, their relief overcoming any anger. It had been a good adventure and now I could enjoy exploring the old farm machinery that lay around everywhere, fishing and bathing in the Brant River, the summer threshing rituals and the occasional excitement of a line-side fire adjoining one of grandad's fields, courtesy of a hard-working D Class 4-4-0 passing on the line that had witnessed my small shame at being over-carried.

There were many other 'firsts', of course. The first time on a locomotive footplate was one, and then the first day of employment by the London & North Eastern Railway, when I travelled the whole journey to St Neots in the brake compartment just to feel I belonged. A short piece I wrote about that day appeared in an issue of the old *LNER Magazine*. Then there was the first time 'in charge', which came after I had moved to the Norwich district.

After a spell at Wells-on-Sea, memorable for having to fix parcel labels on to wet bags of sea fish, I was instructed to relieve the chief booking clerk at Fakenham West. Wow, that sounded good – a position of substance at last! I imagined the early and late turn clerks would carry the job and I could bask in their efforts and make meaningful decisions. Not so; they were even younger and less experienced than I was and, worse, could not manage the single-needle telegraph instrument. I began to wish I had spent more of my time at Eccles Road on the training instrument, but had found more interesting things to do there, including spending time with the signalman and sampling the local Banham Cider Company's offerings.

In those days the telegraph instruments were located in station booking offices in the old Great Eastern area and were the prime source of communication. The staff at the Norwich hub of the system could send messages in Morse at incredible speeds and competent receivers signalled their willingness to accept this by sending 'G' – two long dashes/needle-moves to the right – followed by one short/left, after the preliminaries of repeating their station call sign and holding down the key handle to signify their attention. Unfortunately, I was only a 'T' reader, one who had laboriously to decipher each arriving word and indicate understanding by sending 'T' back. I managed, but took an awful lot of time to do so and stretched the patience of the Norwich staff to breaking point. But they could not win since the receiver could hold up the proceedings at any time by just holding the handle/needle of the instrument still until their anger dissipated.

Sometime after this, as my appreciation of both the professional railway and its origins increased, I earned my first professional writing fee – £2, I think – for an article in *Trains Illustrated* about the Essendine to Bourne branch. I travelled on the last day before closure and this vignette image of a disappearing railway age is still very clear in my mind. Oddly enough, the motive power was a British Railways (BR) Standard 2MT but the two old, quaint saloon coaches were from a different age. The guard was immaculate and complete with traditional rose buttonhole. Any spare time on the short journey he spent polishing the brass fitments of his stock. I just had time to photograph the ancient Red House which served as Bourne station building and was popularly rumoured to be haunted. Back on the platform to take a photograph of the train which would take me back to Essendine, the guard insisted that all his passengers and the train crew should line up to appear in my shot, just the way it had happened in so many early railway photographs. I have written much since then but that first fee was really something.

A Great Crash & a Cloud of Coal Dust

During his duties one evening Hugh Gould came across a wagon with a mind of its own.

In 1952, while a student at Glasgow University, I took a summer job as a porter at Drumchapel station, in the Glasgow North district ex-LNER (NBR) suburban network. I spent my first day on the railway unloading a coal wagon at the behest of the stationmaster, Willie Kirkpatrick, 'to help a good customer avoid demurrage'. Throughout the day I was harangued by the relief porter I was to replace, a left-wing Aberdonian, who insisted that 'they had no right' to make me do that. But I knew a co-operation test when I saw one, and Willie K. and I got on very well afterwards.

Drumchapel goods depot consisted of a single hump siding shunted by a freight trip every weekday morning, usually worked by an Eastfield depot Class J37 locomotive. The only traffics were coal wagons and BD containers for a local biscuit firm. On late duty, I would spend part of the summer evenings tidying up the siding by putting up the wagon doors, using a small hand crane to put the container back on its Conflat wagon, shackling it up and running it down to the bottom of the siding to couple everything ready for a straight lift next morning.

One evening, the Conflat refused to budge, even with the aid of a pinch-bar. Peeved, I went on down to the foot of the siding to put up the wagon doors there. Then I heard a rumbling noise. The Conflat had belatedly decided it was time to go and was accelerating towards me. I ran forward, but could do nothing to halt its relentless progress, only await the consequences. There was a great crash and a cloud of coal dust, but mercifully, no derailment. I coupled up and went back to the booking office, slightly shaken and with a lesson learned.

Next day, the permanent way ganger, a kindly Highlander called Angus McPherson who lived in the stationmaster's house, Willie K. living elsewhere, sidled into the booking office and whispered into my ear: 'I heard you shunting last night, Hughie!'

LMS Apprentice

Alan Sourbut, who retired as chief mechanical & electrical engineer, Eastern Region, recalls his early days as an apprentice fitter, which stood him in good stead in his later career.

It was 7.30 a.m. on 10 May 1943, with snow falling heavily as I commenced my first paid position as an apprentice electrical fitter, following a two-year course at the local technical college. The location was the carriage repair shop at Meols Cop, Southport, the main depot for the electric trains on the Liverpool–Southport and Crossens–Ormskirk lines. The depot covered all maintenance and repairs to this fleet and was staffed by sixty artisans and others. Supervision was by a foreman leading electrician, who clocked on like the other staff and whose clock card showed a base pay rate some four shillings higher than those he supervised. General control of the depot, plus the staff at Hall Road Shed, was under a salaried grade engineer.

There was a clear distinction between the wages grade depot staff and the salaried office staff. Incredibly, when the engineer was not there, the chief clerk, not the foreman, took charge of the shop. The fitters were dual-crafted, mechanical and electrical, and we apprentices learned much from them, including the use of equipment and diagnostic skills. We also suffered their pranks and idiosyncrasies. Initiation varied, but all the lads were sent for the 'long stand' where the victim was

A Class 302 electric multiple unit stands outside Meols Cop depot. (Alan Sourbut)

despatched to the stores and then relayed from one fitter to another and made to wait for some time at each. Eventually, the light would dawn and he would return to his mate to be admonished somewhat impolitely!

There were known dangers at work: the live rails outside the depot could produce a painful experience at 650v, asbestos was used extensively, and heavy bogie work could easily cause injured hands.

After about three years at Meols Cop depot, some time was spent at Hall Road Inspection and Cleaning Shed, fault-finding on trains in service and sometimes on live equipment. Cleaning was done by Italian prisoners of war who arrived, without guards, on a bus. A major was in charge, and he doubled as a cook to those nice guys who revealed wonderful voices as they sang while cleaning the trains. Some of them had artisan skills and borrowed our workshop at times. Many an ashtray on their coach became a cigarette lighter.

Some months were spent at substations and on 'live rail working' where we handled live switches and cables using rubber gloves! Towards the end of the apprenticeship, twelve months were spent at Horwich Works in the machine and electrical shops. This was a location where men had names like Entwistle and Ramsbottom and greeted each other with 'erst goin' on ould fettler' or similar words.

The 6.20 a.m. train from Southport took me to Lostock (Bolton). Then came a bus ride to the works after a steep hill walk. Twice a week I had tea in the works canteen; then I would go by train to Wigan to study for engineering qualifications and home by train to Southport. There I met a girlfriend – now my wife of sixty-two years – and had supper at her home until late. Returning on the 6.20 a.m. train next morning was fine until Wigan, where mill girls joined with lots of shouting and banging – they all wore clogs! There was danger in making careless comments because the pack could be aggressive, as one lad came to experience by losing an item of clothing.

The apprentice scheme was well organised and closely monitored and was a credit to the LMS. When I was 21 I moved on to become a draughtsman in the district office at Liverpool, and the experience of having worked with tools and machines was invaluable. Above all, this had been a great learning process, working alongside skilled men, understanding their pride in doing a good job, and savouring their humour and fellowship. As I moved around the railway industry in a management role, I always felt at home and got on well with those people who represented a key feature of that great enterprise.

The 1987 Hurricane – A Personal Experience

In the early hours of a Friday morning in October 1987, Theo Steel was awakened to deal with the effects of a violent storm on both his railway and his home.

I went to bed on Thursday 15 October 1987 aware that there was a storm in the English Channel; but I was not in the slightest degree prepared for what was about to happen. At the time I was assistant general manager – a short-term co-ordination role in East Anglia, scheduled to end imminently with the creation of the Anglia Region. Indeed, John Edmonds was due to arrive as designate general manager on 19 October.

I was awoken by a telephone call at about 2.30 in the early hours of the Friday morning; it was overhead line engineer John Sills to say that he was out driving and had been almost hit by more than one falling tree. His information from the Electrical Control Centre overhead line monitoring facility at Romford was that they had already recorded more incidents that night than in all the previous thirty-eight years of electrification, and that trying to run any electric trains was impossible. A timescale for repairs was not practicable as we were still in the eye of the storm. We agreed that John should go home, but with caution.

I telephoned the control office at Liverpool Street and gave instructions that trains were to cease moving in East Anglia. At that hour there were no passenger trains on the move but I recall that we had to recess a Freightliner train at Witham and that its driver took a long while to get home. It was clear that movement on any route in East Anglia was going to be perilous, whether electrified or not.

Next I had a conversation with Phyllis Allen who was then our public relations and press manager. I asked her to get in touch with her radio and press contacts.

By now it was around 3.30 a.m. and we were in the thick of the storm at home in Southend. The family all got up, dressed and prepared themselves to leave the house quickly if necessary.

David Rayner, who was general manager at York at the time, got hold of us and was quite incredulous that we had decided to stop all trains and on my head be it. Ironically, there was a huge crash in the middle of this conversation which he could hear and on investigation I realised it was some 600 tiles coming off one end of our roof! A fine demonstration of just what we were facing, and it wasn't over yet. David's switch from incredulity to empathy was immediate, but it did demonstrate just what a surprise the intensity of the storm was. In the event, no East Coast Main Line trains ran south of Peterborough on the Friday, either.

It was now about 6 a.m. and I had to get the germ of a recovery plan together while the storm continued to rage. It stopped suddenly at dawn and we were able to assess the damage to the roof at home which we got battened down later in the day. Luckily the damage was not structural, although there were houses in Southend that were rendered roofless and uninhabitable.

About 9 a.m. I got to the area manager's office at Southend Central with some difficulty and did a telephone round-up there. All agreed that we would aim to get the railway open again for Monday morning and that the plan for damage repair in the electrified area was to work outwards from Central London. I left the various functions to get on with the work and asked to be advised of any problems. I recall that army assistance was offered but not used.

The critical path was going to be tree clearance and restoration of the overhead lines, and I arranged a Saturday morning conference at the Romford Electrical Control Centre to review progress. Key roads were passable by this time although traffic lights were not all working. Our car had not been damaged but our neighbour's had. There was a lot to do but a resumption of the full service on Monday seemed possible and to be aimed for. All the rolling stock was serviceable and had been on live track sections – earlier snows in 1987 had not only interrupted supplies but ruined the traction motors on about fifty units.

The railway was cleared by Sunday afternoon and, indeed, some steam shuttle services on the London, Tilbury & Southend section even ran! Luckily that did not hit the headlines. Actually, the press was not unsympathetic. I resisted the temptation to start services early as this would have hindered the restoration job in hand which was much aided by the assumption that there was no train movement going on.

A full service resumed on Monday 19 October, but the trains ran very late due to a lot of slipping and sliding. The Class 315 units apart, we were still on clasp brakes at the time and the vegetation and autumn leaf fall management was not the issue it became shortly afterwards. For a few weeks we also suffered from a lot of track circuit problems due to salt impregnation. I guess the storm just provided an extreme form of vegetation management! My estimate that 15 per cent of the trees in our Southend road had to be replaced gives some idea of the scale of the storm damage.

As ever in these situations everyone rallied round, and I use this as an opportunity to recognise a good team effort in what turned out to be unique circumstances. The 1987 storm is supposedly a once-in-300-years event, although there was another in January 1990. Records show that nothing like it had been seen since 1703 so it is one of the few unprecedented events that I have been involved in during my railway career.

When our commuters again arrived in London on their restored services, those employed in the financial markets were faced with a 26 per cent fall in the stock market on what became known as Black Monday. So the storm was wider than just the wind!

Slips, Slides & Washouts

In his early days in the district engineer's office at Perth, Jim Dorward learned to expect the unexpected.

It is Thursday 19 November 1959 and I am in the Perth district engineer's office. It is my second year on the long road to becoming a civil engineer. The coal-fired stove is burning well and the office is comfortably warm. District engineer Harry Eagers rings for Permanent Way C – 'God' to us lesser mortals. He was one bell on the boss's special call system. I was much lower down, at least four bells.

The district engineer probably wishes to discuss the latest track subsidence at Thornton Junction on the East Coast Main Line, a location badly affected by the workings of the Fife coalfield; the local permanent way inspector believes that the original station there is buried several feet below the present one. Alternatively, he may be wanting to talk about the design drawings for a junction renewal job that have just come back from the print room in the chief civil engineer's office at Glasgow St Enoch station. These drawings on special linen are sent by passenger train to Glasgow for printing, the round trip taking three days. So mistakes are not permitted!

As it turns out, I am told that I need to be part of a team to go to Dollar, on the line between Alloa and Kinross Junction, to do a survey of a landslide resulting from heavy rain. When we reach the site we can see that it is not a massive landslide and the line can be reopened with just an emergency speed restriction. Little did we realise what the next day would bring in the way of trouble from Mother Nature.

It is now Friday 20 November and when I arrive in the office it is clear from the number of bells ringing that something out of the ordinary has happened. The 6.41 a.m. passenger train from Aberfeldy to Ballinluig has run into a washout near Balnaguard. More rain had fallen overnight and water from two blocked ditches had poured down the hillside towards the single-line railway. The water had washed away the ballast and much of the supporting ground as it swept downwards to the nearby River Tay.

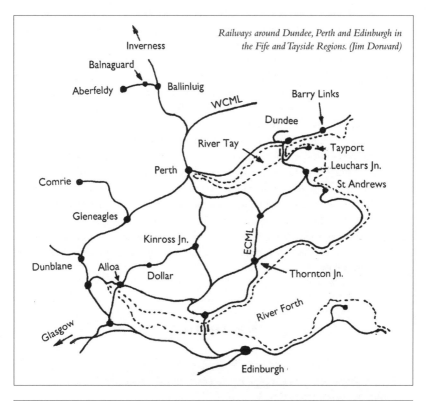

Railways around Dundee, Perth and Edinburgh in the Fife and Tayside Regions. (Jim Dorward)

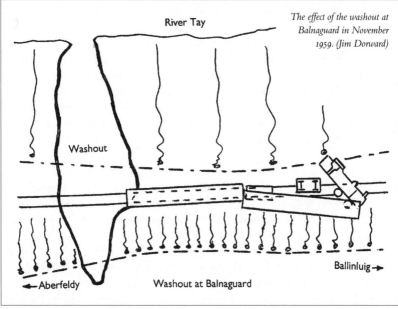

The effect of the washout at Balnaguard in November 1959. (Jim Dorward)

The passenger train had been formed of two coaches hauled by 0-4-4 steam locomotive No. 55218 travelling bunker first. When it reached the washout, the track was already hanging in mid-air. The engine and coaches crossed the hole, pounded up the far side, made the gap much bigger and smashed into the slope of the cutting. Fortunately, the driver and fireman were not seriously hurt but, needless to say, were badly shaken. The guard fell out of the train into the hole and the sole passenger was slightly injured.

There was now a need to survey the site for the production of the accident plan and for the design of the reinstatement work – a new pipe culvert, earthworks and new track. Four from the drawing office, including myself, were despatched by road to Balnaguard. When we got there a television news crew was on site, together with a photographer from the *Dundee Courier*. We appeared on TV that night and in the newspaper the following morning. The subsequent accident report made it clear, to our relief, that the washout was pure mischance, with no one in any way to blame. However, these two days taught me that 'the permanent way' is by no means permanent.

Kettering

Dennis Simmonds recalls some down-to-earth aspects of the goods, parcels and passenger departments at Kettering.

Kettering goods station not only dealt with general goods, but had a substantial business in locally manufactured footwear and in receiving the lasts used for fashioning shoes. The latter came loose in vans and had to be transferred by hand to drays for delivery. For country collections and deliveries there was a motor fleet of three vehicles, but most of the cartage to and from the town area was by the horse-drawn drays. Arrivals of beer were always delivered this way as the free drinks provided by landlords often meant that the horse had to be relied upon to get the dray home.

The stables were a boon to one member of staff. This man played the violin and was known to the other senior clerks, but not to the juniors, as Fiddler Smith. Each day he would bring his sandwiches to work in a tin box. After lunch he would go to the stables and fill the empty tin with horse manure to take home for his garden. Needless to say, he never offered to share his sandwiches!

The Kettering goods shed held about ten wagons and unloading started there at 5 a.m. The junior delivery clerk was rostered to start work at this time, collect the invoices from the passenger station and make out the delivery sheets for the carmen. The documents were marked with a rotary numbering stamp to facilitate tracing. When I was on this early turn my timekeeping was not all it should have been and my main aim was to arrive just before the chief delivery clerk, Harry Ellis, who walked the 4 miles from Burton Latimer to start at 6 a.m. His first action was to check the stamp to see how many sheets I had completed; my first action was to move the stamp forward some thirty or so numbers.

Major freight customers at this time included Weetabix – who had a private siding at Burton Latimer – and Wicksteeds, who made heavy machinery and equipment for children's playgrounds. The Wicksteed family endowed a large local park for public use and fitted it out with slides, roundabouts and swings.

Freight traffic, or goods traffic as we called it back in 1940, was varied and yielded a few perks. The Ever Ready battery agent used to collect his stocks from the station and the staff were allowed to purchase torch batteries, very scarce at the time, from him. Occasionally, packages of goods must have split open during handling for I remember one occasion when both my jacket pockets were stuffed with Liquorice Allsorts.

I had a short spell in the parcel office where there was a habit of creating perks if fortune did not provide them. The communal tea fund got its treats from the careless handling of biscuits and cakes, especially Cadbury's mini chocolate rolls. Another dubious practice was to get our milk supply from one of the considerable number of 20-gallon churns brought in by farmers for despatch to the local dairy. A near-forgotten feature of railway parcel offices was the ubiquitous pot of smelly brown glue used to stick on luggage destination labels and parcel value stamps or ledger labels.

After a short time on parcels I was moved to the booking office, a busy place with two ticket windows into the booking hall and the rest of that wall filled with ticket racks. These held the printed ticket stock for the most frequently used destinations, blank tickets being completed by hand for others. Special types of ticket were held for service personnel, 'privilege' tickets – always referred to as 'privs' – for the reduced rate travel of railway staff, and 'zone' tickets for prams, bicycles and dogs. A portion of a ticket, known as the 'snip', was removed and retained when a printed ticket was issued for a child. Commercial travellers had books of vouchers which could be used for reduced fare tickets. Other groups with special ticketing arrangements included HM Forces travelling on duty, circus hands and performers, theatre staff accompanying scenery, grooms in horseboxes, blind people, prisoners under police escort and so on. The Coaching Arrangements Book was the bible for all these facilities.

At the end of his shift each of the three junior clerks had to balance the tickets issued with the cash taken. This meant relating the number of the last unissued ticket at the bottom of the tube to the number at the end of the previous shift and multiplying the number sold by the appropriate fare. All the other types of earnings were treated this way and the total, hopefully, balanced with the money taken. Excess fares, cloakroom and lavatory receipts and many other items might have to be included, depending on the functions and scope of each station's booking office.

Sometimes, under the pressure of issuing tickets quickly to a large and impatient queue of would-be travellers, mistakes would occur. These might just be failing to record a blank card destination, intending to do so as soon as the queue had gone. Worse were the occasions when a tube ran empty and the batch of replacement tickets were not matched for sequence with the previous ones, producing a substantial 'loss in booking' until the error was spotted and rectified.

Being a principal station on the Midland Main Line there was always a great deal going on. In addition to the passenger services, there were numerous trainloads of heavy freight passing through, especially coal from the coalfields of the Derby–Nottingham area. This traffic was carried on Toton-Brent services, worked by Beyer-Garrett articulated locomotives. These were 2-6-6-2 monsters which could move ninety wagons of coal or a hundred empty wagons. On one occasion, one of these coal trains was diverted into a siding at Wigston to allow a fast train to pass. The brakes failed to stop the train in time and the leading pair of pilot wheels dropped off the rails into a sandpit. After the wagons had been detached, the breakdown crew came to recover the derailed locomotive by attaching a Class 8 freight locomotive to the rear to draw it backwards. The unfortunate result was that the Garrett's drawbar snapped under the strain. Some typical breakdown crew's ingenuity was then needed to recover it by less conventional means. In the end, the crippled engine had to be taken to Wellingborough locomotive depot with one Class 8 pushing it and two in front to stop it.

Iron ore was mined in our area. Prior to the war major steelworks in Scotland had been closed, throwing huge numbers of employees out of work. When Stewarts & Lloyds opened a new steelworks at Corby, a few miles from Kettering, this became a Scottish enclave with hundreds of experienced steelworkers moving there to staff the new enterprise.

Some of the iron ore mined in our area went to steelworks other than Corby. A mine on the Nottingham line despatched ore to a works on the Leicester line. This travelled via Glendon Junction, north of Kettering, where the right-hand fork of the main line went to Nottingham and the left-hand one to Leicester and Derby. To simplify the working the train locomotive propelled its train to and over the junction so that it was at the right end to haul it on its journey. Normally this manoeuvre was carried out without difficulty, but in one notable incident the necessary precaution of attaching the propelling locomotive to its train was overlooked. The guard, who was in his brake van at what was temporarily the front of the train, realised that it was moving too fast and hurriedly screwed on his handbrake. When this failed to slow the train he leapt from the brake van on to the line side. Freed of its locomotive and its guard the runaway picked up speed down the 1 in 118 gradient south of the junction and ran for some 10 miles before a half-mile rise on the approach to Wellingborough halted its startling progress.

Renaissance 4472

Steam traction on British Railways was in its last years, but Bryan Stone had a hand in its revival as a liaison for Alan Pegler's pioneering rescue of No. 4472.

In September 2011 I saw an obituary. George Hinchcliffe, once chairman of the Steam Locomotive Operators' Association, had died at the age of 89. I remember George in my office at Doncaster's Gresley House in the mid-1960s, I a young passenger manager, he a schoolmaster from Gainsborough. We spent many hours together.

In January 1963 *The Times* had portrayed *Flying Scotsman*, No. 60103 as it was then, in the sunlit snow on its last BR train. At Doncaster it was sold to Alan Pegler of the Northern Rubber Company, Retford, and a member of the Eastern Region Board. It was lightly overhauled at his expense, restored to 1930s style in LNER green, and, under a private contract valid to 1972, operated from April 1963 on special trains.

George Hinchcliffe was the president of the Gainsborough Model Railway Society and had already run special trains with unusual engines. He became Alan's '4472' manager, and so Alan and George came to me, the nominated interface with the 'real railway'. They ran 4472, as she had again become, as often as they could, with all sorts of schemes.

At that period we still had steam in many places, though with gaps, and some practical difficulties had to be solved. Was 4472 safe? BR engineers and especially boiler inspectors took care of her. She was housed in a little shed by the Plant Works,

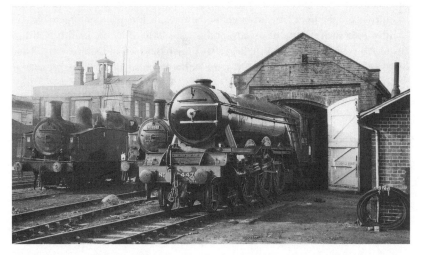

No. 4472 Flying Scotsman *stands in the small depot which Alan Pegler rented at Doncaster Plant Works, flanked by the works' departmental J50s. (Bryan Stone)*

and they knew all about Class A3 Pacifics. Was she within gauge and locomotive route availability limits? Increasingly difficult, could she be watered and turned? And what would it all cost? Remember, this was the first private engine to run in this way with BR providing rolling stock and train crews, and Alan paying for engine, fuel and water. We had no idea of track access costs, and neither did the civil engineer. The main elements were staff costs, empty running, signal box special openings, inspectors and station costs. All over Britain I sought information, confirmation and costs. Special timetables would need to emerge.

Finally, we drew up a standard contract, which listed the particular day's events, added up the numbers, thought of a (substantial) margin and proposed a price. George and Alan were not people to be misled, so we usually agreed quickly. Then the arrangements were published and made to work.

The trips were hugely successful; thousands travelled. But it got more difficult as time went on. The retreat of steam meant fewer facilities available, fewer staff and a much bigger nuisance factor. Morale generally was falling and many parts of BR were unhelpful: 'Don't send that thing here!' Alan fitted an extra 6,000-gallon corridor tender to ease the problems and we had a great fortieth anniversary of 4472's London–Edinburgh non-stop run of 1 May 1928.

Did I get any trips? In May 1967 I was on a Doncaster to Norwich excursion, via the Joint Line and Ely, which led the Great Eastern section, which had had no steam for years, a merry dance. Wrong line running was needed, and reversing on Thorpe triangle, as well as a diesel pilot engine, and more! Oh yes, there was a night back in 1964 when Alan invited me to ride 4472 light engine from London to Doncaster after a special. With the office footplate pass I joined a Deltic to King's Cross and waited. I was soon aboard 4472 and off for inspection at Hornsey, before turning on the Canonbury triangle. It was a quiet night, though at Grantham we were diverted to Lincoln and the Joint Line, and I got home at 6 a.m. It remains unforgettable.

After 1967 such private steam adventures were stopped by the British Railways Board. Alan's contract was only upheld after a fight. But I left in December 1968 and only saw him and George once more, at the author Freeman Allen's funeral years later.

First Course

On-going training was a normal part of developing railway managers. Geoff Body found residential course content both practical and intense, but there were lighter moments.

After some time in my first permanent post after traffic apprentice training I was sent on a junior management course. For me it was the first residential course I had been on and the attractive venue, a former mansion near Windsor used primarily for training BR novice chefs, seemed a good augury. The arrival afternoon involved the usual settling-in process and, after a comfortable night, I headed for the elegant breakfast room prepared to be delighted by the kitchen's best efforts.

I had not counted on us being joined by some extremely senior and august railway notables who intended, I had no doubt, to keep an eye on our social deportment and fitness to progress. Well brought up, I thoughtfully passed the sugar bowl to a future chairman only to see the tongs, which had been perched on top, execute a graceless dive into the milk jug with accompanying 'plop' and splashes. Abject apologies should have closed the incident but I had not noticed that my solid breakfast knife was lying with its handle protruding from the edge of the table. With my returning elbow I caught it sharply and watched in horror as it somersaulted noisily across the dining room. Now it was not only my table companions who were staring!

I remember nothing else of that course and, hopefully, no one remembered me.

The Battle of Broughty Ferry

Harry Knox recalls the incredible tribulations of trying to modernise a traditional, ageing level crossing at Broughty Ferry, near Dundee.

Gray Street Level Crossing, Broughty Ferry

It all started when we had to modernise the level crossing at Gray Street, Broughty Ferry, between Dundee and Arbroath. Until 1966, the design and layout of the crossing had remained virtually unchanged. It comprised four wooden gates which swung alternately across the road and across the railway, being prevented from swinging outwards towards the road by cast-iron stops in the roadway. These gate stops were operated by a lever in the signal box and were mechanically locked and interlocked with the signalling arrangements. When the operating capstan wheel in the signal box was wound, the gates swung simultaneously by means of interconnected mechanical cranks and rodding, driven by the wheel.

Broughty Ferry signal box was an exceptional three storeys high above rail level; thus, the gate operating linkage was much longer and heavier than normal and much greater effort was required to turn the wheel. The linkage, due to the great complexity, was also subject to heavy wear and tear. This complicated mechanical rodding was required to be run below the road surface, encased in wooden channels. The length of the linkage and a slight curvature of the railway through the crossing caused a slight distortion of the road profile, rendering motor vehicles liable to underside damage if due care and speeds were not observed.

Broughty Ferry LNER station back in gas lamp days. The problem level crossing is at the far end of the platform, with the three-storey signal box adjacent to the white signal sighting board. (Harry Knox)

A Long, Sad Story Unfolds

The heavy wear and tear on the complex crossing mechanism meant that by October 1966 it had become life-expired. Under the 1957 Level Crossing Act, which permitted the replacement of gated crossings by new, electrically operated half- or full-barrier crossings and protecting road traffic lights, a scheme was drawn up by BR to replace the gates at Broughty Ferry with such an installation. Due notice was given to both the Dundee Corporation and the police authorities at a site meeting in October 1966. The corporation signified approval and a draft Section 66 Order was lodged with the Scottish Development Department. No objections were made in the ensuing statutory two-month period.

Then, in February 1967, the corporation belatedly intimated an objection, which was duly referred to the minister. They had received a deputation from the townspeople, who had expressed concern at the ease of access to the railway allowed by the new barrier installations. BR provided all the information and evidence to support the case for barriers to Inspecting Officer of Railways, Major Peter Olver, who after due consideration decided that the corporation concerns were unfounded and the objection was withdrawn.

It was at this point that the Dundee Corporation decided to question BR's statutory right to replace gates with barriers, suggesting that doing so would be contrary to the original Dundee & Arbroath Railway Act of 1836. Advised that the 1957 Act overrode the 1836 one, the corporation once more questioned the validity of Section 66 of the former.

Time marched on without progress until 1972, when the deteriorating condition of the crossing gave BR no option but to renew it on a like-for-like basis. Fortunately, enough design expertise remained within the regional signal and telegraph drawing office to permit this option.

The Second Attempt

The next attempt to modernise the crossing was in 1985 when its condition was again causing concern, necessitating its inclusion in the 1986/87 Signalling Infrastructure Renewal Programme for replacement with a CCTV-controlled barrier crossing. At a site meeting held on 7 May 1986 I, as ScotRail operations signalling & safety officer, outlined the proposals for the crossing renewal, as required by law, to all interested parties. We were then notified by the representatives of the district council (successor to the corporation) that, without any notification to us, the level crossing had been included in the existing Grade B listing for Broughty Ferry station, signal box and overbridge. The reason given was that Gray Street contained much 'Victorian ambience' and was thus environmentally sensitive.

We intended to appeal the listing and, in an attempt to allay fears of environmental vandalism, ScotRail invited district and regional councils and other appropriate bodies to nominate one member each to visit an existing crossing of the type proposed, located in a truly historical and environmentally sensitive setting: St Dunstan's level crossing in the heart of Canterbury. The trip duly took place but did not produce a change of heart in everyone.

Round Three

The modernisation plans lay in the doldrums until November 1986 when again I tabled our intentions in considerably greater detail. Tayside Constabulary, nonetheless, maintained their concerns regarding risk to pedestrians, while the district council planning officials challenged our legal right to change a listed structure, this despite the fact that the elected regional and district councillors by now actually supported the proposal. In that same month BR was invited by the district council to submit a request for Listed Building Consent to modernise the crossing, which we did in March 1987.

The submission was due to be heard at the April meeting of the Dundee District Development Committee, but one week after the application was submitted, and before any meeting took place, the *Dundee Courier* newspaper carried a statement made by the leader of the council saying the application would definitely be refused. Refusal was duly confirmed at the April meeting.

BR appealed to the Secretary of State for Scotland against this refusal and a public inquiry was convened in November 1989. It was chaired by a Scottish Office reporter and I, on behalf of BR, led the evidence as to why the crossing was now archaic and rapidly deteriorating, arguing it was unrealistic to expect BR to maintain and upkeep what was to all intents and purposes a museum piece on a main-line railway.

In December 1989 a serious engineering event occurred at the crossing due to the deteriorating condition and wear and tear of the gates. One gate slipped off the stop as a train was passing and the ensuing damage to the infrastructure demanded that we secured the gates across the roadway, thereby closing Gray Street to through traffic. Real life had intervened in the convoluted administrative processes taking place.

In January 1990 the reporter published his findings and upheld that the crossing was an integral part of the Victorian Building Group and should be included in the Category B list. His findings incorporated an unacceptable recommendation that BR should undertake repairs to sort out the profile of the roadway and improve the crossing surface; this despite the fact that in listing the crossing, the roadway between the gates was by association also listed.

It was made crystal clear to all concerned that complying with the reporter's dubious instruction to re-profile the crossing would entail the removal of the wooden linkage channels, thus rendering the crossing wholly inoperable. Despite this, the planning department intimated that there would be no shift in their stance and the gates must be retained. I felt compelled to ask them where in the listing it actually specified that the gates should be maintained 'in working order', a point they had to concede.

Road Closed

The damaged gates were duly secured across the road, effectively closing it, but we were soon under pressure from both regional and district councils to have the road reopened as soon as possible. With the operating linkage now rendered inoperable, the difficulties in achieving safe reopening were fully explained to all on several occasions, but this went unheeded. However, by now, the Community Council and the Business Group in Broughty Ferry were making it clear that they favoured modernisation and as quickly as possible.

In August 1990 BR decided to promote a Provisional Order to achieve a permanent road closure and so advised Tayside Regional Council. They came back with a quite extraordinary response, stating that since ScotRail owned the portion of roadway between the gates, they also had the absolute right to close off the road at will. High farce indeed!

A Backward Step

In October 1990 the crossing was reopened, with the road surface re-profiled and no channels. Since the signalman could no longer physically operate the gates, a gatekeeper was provided to hand operate them. This method of working was agreed to, as a temporary measure, by HM Inspecting Officer, Major Tony King, but very reluctantly because interlocking between running signals and gates no longer existed and the opportunity for mistakes was obvious. A solution had to be found and hopes were pinned on obtaining a permanent road closure.

Inevitably, an accident occurred, due to the complete failure of communication between crossing keeper and signalman one late afternoon. A southbound High Speed Train (HST), running under clear signals, ran through the gates – which had not been opened – and destroyed most of the level crossing infrastructure, fortunately without any injuries. A major crisis was upon us. Gray Street was once more closed off and the Draft Provisional Order seeking powers to authorise permanent closure was deposited on 27 March 1991. A change of mind by the local planners resulted in them withdrawing all objections to modernisation, overlooking the fact that the Secretary of State was now involved in the listing row.

Success at Last

A commissioners' hearing, chaired by four members of the House of Lords, began on 7 March 1994 and lasted a week. It was music to my ears when, on a site visit, Lord Palmer and his fellow commissioners declared that never again should such an archaic method of working be contemplated and that Broughty Ferry level crossing, if retained, must meet all modern parameters and be replaced by full barriers and road traffic lights. They duly ruled that Gray Street be reopened once a new CCTV-controlled barrier level crossing could be provided.

At the end of that month I departed for a new career in railway consultancy. Railtrack took over from 1 April and, building on the commissioners' ruling, went the whole hog, closing Broughty Ferry and Barry East signal boxes and putting signalling and level crossing control into Dundee Signalling Centre.

And so ended the long, sad saga of Broughty Ferry, which was quite unique in railway circles. Nowhere else was a level crossing ever 'listed', although in the south one council later went a step further and listed semaphore running signals … but that's another story.

A Shuttle Cock-Up

Cedric Spiller watched what should have been good public relations go badly awry at Paddington.

The title of this piece became an infamous headline in the sports section of the *Guardian* newspaper in the late 1980s, referring to a total breakdown of train arrangements, communication and a few other unhappy events on the Western Region of BR.

The previous day, as national products manager for the British Railways Board, I had launched a nationwide tour of professional badminton players at Paddington station. We built a full-sized badminton court on The Lawn, as the station concourse has long been known, in order for the media to film and photograph the occasion. It was seen as 'a good PR opportunity'. However, such high-profile events can rapidly turn into bad PR, which is precisely what happened on this occasion.

To satisfy the needs of the BBC, ITN and the media in general it was arranged for a giant shuttlecock to be attached to the front of the early morning High Speed Train from Swansea. In addition, the lead power car would be specially cleaned and painted. The press were geared up for its dramatic arrival at 11 a.m. Contact with WR Control indicated that the train was on time and yours truly proudly announced to the cameras that its arrival was imminent on platform 3.

Consternation! What came into sight was not an impressive, sparkling giant shuttlecock, but the filthiest HST power car you have ever seen, and no shuttle at all! Needless to say, the media were not amused. Next day they had a field day. Not only did the *Guardian* carry the strong headline 'What a Shuttle Cock-Up', but the first Sir Bob Reid (BR's chairman) remarked to me, 'Well, you certainly cocked that up.' The final comment went to Conrad, the stationmaster at Paddington at the time, who was heard to mutter to the media, 'heads will roll'. Thankfully, mine was not one of them.

Tales of a Young Controller

The control offices dealt with the day-to-day running of the railway system with all its vagaries and complications. Nick Wood recalls a few of the latter from his control days.

In mid-1960, after eighteen months in the New England yardmaster's office at Peterborough, and on the advice of assistant yard masters Harry Goodchild and George Nunn, I found myself in King's Cross control office as a Class 4 assistant controller. I was then aged 18½ and I went there with Pat Haynes, a signal box lad from Huntingdon South. With the closure of the London Midland Region Peterborough Control it had been intended to transfer the responsibility for the lines between Kings Dyke and Luffenham/Thrapston/Seaton to the King's Cross number four section controller, and we were to assist. In the event, the responsibility went to Cambridge Control but we were retained at King's Cross and learnt the 'back desk', which involved recording the punctuality of all the East Coast Main Line expresses and Class C freight trains, giving and receiving all the freight train loadings to Doncaster and Lincoln Controls, and providing assistance as required by the deputy chief controller.

I saw and was involved in, to a greater or lesser extent, the congestion which occurred at King's Cross on summer Saturdays and at other busy or difficult periods. There were hot boxes, engine failures, freezing fog, heavy snow, derailments, signal and point failures, etc. – all too numerous to mention, but one or two incidents stand out from this period of my career.

One blustery Saturday afternoon in September 1961 I came on duty expecting a quiet shift. It was not to be. The royal family had come in their special train from Scotland to attend a funeral near Hitchin and planned to return by air. The empty royal train was to return to Peterborough en route to Wolverton, where it was kept when not required. The train arrived punctually at Hitchin and the royal party departed for the funeral. The empty stock was ready to depart well before time and the operating superintendent in Hitchin Yard Box instructed us to despatch it. So we did. However, shortly after the stock had left we received a call from an equerry saying the royal family could not return by air due to the prevailing weather conditions and would return by train instead.

By now the stock was approaching Biggleswade so the signalman at Sandy was instructed to stop it and send it back to Hitchin. A special 'royal' running under 'Grove' conditions had to be hastily arranged involving the Great Northern line traffic manager's control office at King's Cross, York Regional Control and all the relevant district control offices. The number of people who had to be advised and called out again, even in our area, was significant and DCC Sid Mills allocated all us controllers, irrespective of responsibility, a list of people to contact. It all went well: the royal family left Hitchin for Scotland without an apparent hitch, but we had an extremely busy afternoon.

Still young and green, but with some fifteen months' toil on the 'back desk' behind me, I was horrified to be told one morning by the DCC – the vastly experienced Alec Brown – that I would be the number three section controller the following week on nights. I protested that I didn't 'know the job', but that cut no ice with him and he said I could have two days' worth of 'learning' and if anything really serious happened he would step in. In any case, 'the quickest way to learn a job was to do it' was his maxim. After a couple of nights and getting over considerable nervousness, I began to enjoy myself, receiving the regular reports from the signalmen on the passage of trains and, when appropriate, undertaking a bit of train regulation. It was a quiet week, just the odd 'seven bells' for a hot box and a small problem at Hitchin with the overnight King's Cross to York parcels train.

All this lulled me into a false sense of security. On the Saturday morning, just after 6 a.m., Connington South reported the punctual passing of 1A77, the Aberdeen to King's Cross sleeper. I was just about to ring Huntingdon South to get the time the express passed there when the Abbots Ripton signalman came on the line. I knew something was wrong straightaway because in the normal course of events this signalman never reported to control. My heart turned over when he said: '1A77 is a complete failure at the Wood Walton autos.' I called out in some panic to the DCC who immediately turned to the Peterborough section controller and asked the whereabouts of 1053, the New England–Welwyn Garden City Class C freight. 'Just passing Yaxley,' was the reply.

The exchange continued: 'What engine does it have?'

'A New England V2.'

'Get the Holme signalman,' the DCC then told me.

Holme was instructed to shunt the freight and send its V2 Class 2-6-2 light to Connington South, to be signalled up the goods road to Abbots Ripton and there to set back on the Up Main with a wrong line order on to the front of the stranded 1A77. All this happened and in due course the Abbots Ripton signalman reported that 1A77 was 'on the move', eventually passing him with sparks shooting out of the chimney of the V2 – not surprising given that behind the tender was a dead Deltic and twelve heavy sleeping cars. All this was a salutary experience for this young controller.

Then, of course, there was the unauthorised use of motive power – not by me, I hasten to add – otherwise known as using your initiative to 'keep the job going'. In May 1963 the wooden bridge over the River Nene at Stanground, between Peterborough East and March, was severely damaged by fire and had to be temporarily closed to traffic until repairs could be effected. This resulted in the termination of the freight trains from the LMR at Westwood sidings and the sending of the engines to New England loco depot for servicing before working back to their home depots. At the time we were short of power at New England and it was surprising the number of occasions when these London Midland engines reportedly suffered from defective brick arches or were in need of other repairs at New England. All went well until a railway enthusiast reported to the railway press his surprise at seeing a Stanier 8F 2-8-0 working a New England to Barford power station coal train up the Great Northern Main Line! The LM were not best pleased with us kidnapping their engines and the practice had to cease.

Ever heard of the unauthorised use of a Deltic on the Cambridge Buffet Express? Well, it did happen and a lot of knuckles were rapped after the event.

Out and home partially fitted freight train workings were introduced in the late 1950s between New England and Ferme Park. The outward run took forty to forty-five wagons of coal and returned with a train of empties – up to sixty – using 9F locomotives. The Up direction trains were allocated numbers 1027, 1129 and 1149. It was one of the assistant controllers' responsibilities to record the punctuality of these services.

On arrival at Ferme Park the locomotive would go to Top Shed for turning and servicing. During the week it was not unusual for these trains to lose their booked path and arrive in Ferme Park up to two hours late, with a consequential effect on the return working. However, on Saturdays the signalmen along the route would ask control if the 'Posh' (Peterborough United Football Club) were playing at home. If they were: 'I'll give him a run, then.' In these circumstances the return workings often arrived back in New England up to two hours early. I wonder why!

After a spell in the GN line traffic manager's control at King's Cross and, following reorganisation, in the Eastern Regional control at Liverpool Street, I returned to King's Cross divisional control as a relief controller in the autumn of 1965. I eventually became a number one section controller, covering at that time King's Cross to Wood Green and Bounds Green, including both Up and Down yards at Ferme Park. Shortly afterwards, if my memory serves me correctly, the National Freight Train Plan was implemented and the working at Ferme Park was considerably changed. Under the plan, all the fitted express freights ran to and from Temple Mills and called at Ferme Park only to detach (in the Up direction) and attach (in the Down) the King's Cross traffic.

One evening I had just relieved my colleague when the Down side yard inspector reported that when the portion from King's Cross was added to the portion from Temple Mills he had 'too many for the York goods'. I asked him how many was too many; two or three was the answer. Not wishing to delay the traffic for twenty-four hours, I said 'put them on'. Fifteen minutes later the York guard spoke to me and said the train was five over the length limit. As the train was ready to go, I authorised him to take it, giving my name at his request for entry into his journal. The train left on time and made rapid progress northwards. Once the glow of self-righteousness had subsided, I realised what I had done. No problem for the King's Cross Division because all the diversionary routes were goods or slow lines, but the length limit was there because of the loops in the Doncaster Division north of Grantham. This train only stopped briefly on the main line at Peterborough for crew relief and to put it into New England to detach the five vehicles would impose considerable delay.

So what to do? Appeal to the DCC for a decision? At the time he and the Peterborough section controller were dealing with a serious fire on an Up freight near Essendine, so would not welcome my problem. So I rang Doncaster Control at the destination end direct and asked to speak to the DCC there. Fortunately, he was the highly experienced Alf Crosby whom I had met. I told him who I was and explained the circumstances, accepting responsibility. He said he would see what he could do. For two weeks afterwards I waited for the summons from Bill Stirling, our operating officer, expecting my control career to be over. I don't know what Alf Crosby did, but the summons never came and I am eternally grateful to him.

Wormit & Lochee

For Jim Dorward of the district engineer's office at Perth two successive days meant two accident drawings and two vastly different situations.

It is Sunday 28 May 1961. It is a fine day and I am on the Edinburgh–Perth line between Inverkeithing (near the Forth Bridge) and Rosyth Halt. I am setting out formation, drainage and track levels, along with track alignment pegs, during a 'possession' for the complete renewal of the Down line. Everything is going well. The permanent way inspector on the job is one of those inspectors who likes to get involved in the theoretical side of the work, so we from the drawing office have to be on our toes.

The cranes, excavators, ballast trains and weather are all behaving themselves. The old bullhead track has been loaded on the first ballast train, the dirty old ballast is now on the second train and the one with the new flat bottom track is about to enter the 'possession'. The alignment pegs have been checked, so my contribution to the work is over. However, while I am planning my journey home to Dundee, word comes through that the 1.25 p.m. diesel multiple unit from Tayport to Dundee (Tay Bridge) has 'come off the road' at Wormit station, near the south end of the Tay Bridge.

I immediately recall the terrible accident that occurred at that station exactly six years previously, on the eve of the national rail strike. A Sunday School special train with over 500 passengers, hauled by a Black 5 locomotive, No. 45458, travelling tender first, took the 20mph curve at the station at around 50mph, became derailed and spread itself over the platforms and track as it left Wormit Tunnel. A neighbour of ours, who was travelling on the footplate irregularly, was killed.

I am sent by road to Wormit to do an accident plan. When I reach the site the Dundee section permanent way inspector tells me that 'it was not our fault' – always one of our immediate concerns. He says the train probably passed the Tay Bridge South Outer Home signal at danger, travelled right through the tunnel and derailed itself at the trap points in the station that protect the East Coast Main Line. My survey does not take long so I am soon on my way home by walking over the Tay Bridge – at 2 miles the longest railway bridge in Europe.

It is now the next day, Monday 29 May, and I am in the district engineer's drawing office at Perth preparing two accident plans: one for Wormit and one as a result of a lengthman being killed on the previous Friday at Ninewells Junction, the start of the Dundee & Newtyle Railway.

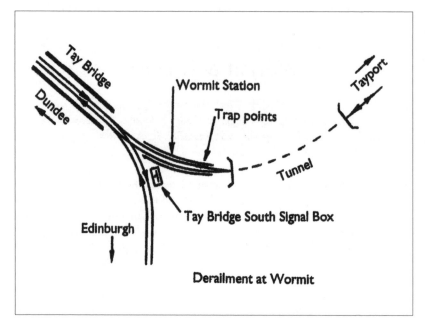

Derailment at Wormit

Except on college days I travel in each day by train from Dundee (West). Near where I live with my parents is the Dundee & Newtyle Railway, a pioneer line which in its original form opened in 1831. The nearest station is Lochee, a pretty, two-platform affair which still looks as it did when the line closed to passenger trains in January 1955. Before that the first train to run through to Blairgowrie had been at 4.36 p.m.!

After I finish my two drawings I am asked to assist a senior engineer with work he is doing in connection with Lochee. He says we have to work out the cost of two new platforms, a new footbridge and a new station building. I am taken aback. Has the local campaign for the reinstatement of service made progress? Or is he confusing Lochee with somewhere else? Lochgelly, perhaps, which is to have a royal train departure quite soon. I ask a leading question: 'Should I go to the plan room for the general arrangements drawing for [with emphasis] *Lochee*?' He says that would be very useful. He is definitely talking about closed Lochee, and is obviously determined to rebuild the place.

Amid total confusion on my part I pluck up the courage to question this engineer (the one who once said I should go to classes to improve my printing on drawings) and ask the obvious question: 'Since Lochee lost its passenger train service a few years ago, why are we working out the cost of what looks like a new station?'

'Ah,' he says. 'It's these accountants at head office in Glasgow. They need to know what it costs to put back any redundant asset that we engineers take away, to keep their books straight.'

I say to myself, 'I'll stick to just keeping the track straight.'

Music: Orchestra & Chorus

Bill Parker reveals something of the serious attitude towards good music-making on the railways, one of many areas of officially supported leisure activity.

The Welsh had their famous colliery choirs and brass bands; so, too, did the many other coalfields. Throughout the UK large companies – notably the manufacturing industries – had their internationally famous brass bands: Fairey Aviation and Black Dyke Mills, for example. All the armed forces had superb bands and the railways did not lag behind. The old railway companies and subsequently the BR Regions, BRB HQ itself and several areas all had their music societies, symphony orchestras and choirs, all of an extremely high musical standard.

What, as an ardent, professional railwayman, was my interest? I had the privilege of getting an excellent musical foundation in my early years, followed by choral training in top-class choirs, orchestral tuition with symphony orchestras and brass bands, and the music direction of several amateur operatic societies. In addition to being a major pleasure in my life, music proved an excellent ambassador for the railways themselves.

The Eastern Region's symphony orchestra was very good, conducted by a competent BBC Symphony Orchestra player. I, as King's Cross divisional manager, had the enjoyable duty of attending their concerts and taking along valuable customers and contacts as guests.

I recall receiving a phone call one morning from the secretary of the orchestra asking me, if I was free, to come to the rehearsal that afternoon. I was needed to replace a percussionist who had called in sick. I thoroughly enjoyed myself, banging the drums and crashing the cymbals, especially after a few nods of approval from the conductor. I was, however, sorry I missed the concert proper as the regular percussionist returned from his sickbed.

My first encounter with music on the railways was with the London-based Eastern Region chorus when I was a district inspector at King's Cross. I 'persuaded' the conductor of the chorus to allow me and my future wife, a fine singer, to join the choir with only two rehearsals available before the concert on the basis we had sung all the music before. The choir comprised members from all grades and all departments, drawn from this large catchment area – and some were better singers than others. They were extremely nice people but it was, nonetheless, quite evident at our first rehearsal that we had been situated between the conductor's 'spies' – which was not unreasonable; we had to be assessed. The rehearsals were well run and the conductor was a professional choir-trainer, despite a tendency during fast, loud bits to act like a windmill in a high wind. The choir produced a good musical standard overall and gave a pleasing concert, despite an extra hallelujah in the small pause near the end of the *Hallelujah Chorus*, and *The Long Day Closes* closing a bit too soon! But the packed audience in the Bishopsgate Institute rendered us generous applause.

I was able to promote the industry in musical circles and, as the musical director of several amateur operatic societies, took every opportunity to push the railway business and act, where necessary, as an unofficial complaints defuser. My colleagues and the senior regional management at York were supportive of my musical involvements. BRB chairman Sir Peter Parker even labelled me 'the electric conductor' in a combined reference to my music and the GN electric service in my division.

With another society I had the privilege of conducting the Band of the Scots Guards at a public concert where the society's chorus performed with them. At this event, I found the director of music and some of his bandsmen were railway enthusiasts, and included the musical piece *The Coronation Scot* in the programme largely for my benefit. I was permitted to conduct this and the choral items at the concert and enjoyed the director's subsequent comment, 'for a railwayman you're not a bad musician'. When my pale-faced wife told my professional musician father-in-law that I would be conducting, his more earthy comment was to the effect of, 'a band of that calibre would play brilliantly even if a monkey was in front conducting!'

My divisional passenger manager, Roland Harman, and I used my musical background as an introduction when we met the organisers – including the bishop and master of music – of the Peterborough City and Cathedral Music and Arts Festival. I knew the master of music and had had a few plays on the cathedral organ. I had also occasionally provided the railway enthusiast bishop with cab passes for journeys to London. I think this liaison helped to influence the decision to use the railway for publicity and as a joint ticketing venue for the festival.

I had the pleasure of attending Christmas railway services in a musical capacity at St Botolph's, Bishopsgate, where I was permitted to play the organ, having had regular lessons there when I worked in the Bishopsgate offices. Especially enjoyable were similar events Doncaster divisional manager Ken Taylor organised at St James, Hexthorpe, which was known as the 'railway church'. I played the organ there, too, with the Salvation Army Band, the drummer of which was Ken's public relations officer. I could not see the players in my mirror, but had no trouble keeping synchronised with the band due to the prominent and bouncy rhythm from the bass and side drums.

There were many other exceptionally good railwaymen musicians, including Alan Sourbut, James Crowe and Roger Williams, who got me an introduction to the master of music and his organ colleagues at York Minster. And that legend, Cambridge district operating superintendent Georgie Sutcliffe – well before my time – was a leading light and secretary of the Cambridge University Music Society. On the theatrical stage I recall the principal tenor of Welwyn Garden City Operatic Society, Bill Taylor, who had a similar active role in the London Railway Operatic Society which had performed at the Scala Theatre in Soho (not Milan); also, Tommy Pepper of Doncaster DSO staff section who was principal comedy actor of the local operatic society, and also the head of the Bishopsgate ER HQ accident section. And there were many more railway folk actively involved in all aspects of music.

During my railway years I heard many excellent choral concerts given by railway societies throughout the network, but the most outstanding one was performed by the York & District Male Voice Choir in York University concert hall in the early 1980s. It was a superb concert of music-making and I am certain that the former conductor of the LNER Music Society, the eminent Leslie Woodgate of the BBC, would have been very satisfied and proud of such an ensemble.

My experience, and that of many others, confirms the wealth of talented music-makers who worked on the railway, and who performed in public and enhanced the image of our industry.

Music: Opera

Unlike Bill Parker in the previous piece, Geoff Body's musical highlight occurred in a valley in Forest Fawr.

Unlike my school friend and subsequent colleague Bill Parker, I had no formal musical training. I agonised my way through songs like *Cherry Ripe* at junior school, sang hymns in a host of Bedfordshire Methodist chapels and was later a member of the King's Cross choir that Bill mentions. I remember enjoying participation in the *Easter Hymn* in London's Guildhall and some externally cold but inwardly warming Christmas carol renderings to homeward-bound commuters on Fenchurch Street station.

Via a friend's introduction to a memorable Beethoven Piano Concerto No. 5 in the Albert Hall and another's revealing analysis of some of the Mozart symphonies, I went to the latter's operas and developed a total commitment to that art form. But where is the railway connection, you ask? In the mid-1960s I moved from the Western Region's West of England Division to take over from Ivor James as area manager for the south-west area of Freightliners Ltd. We had major terminals at Southampton, Cardiff and Swansea, later some mini-terminals and a lot of trade in shipping traffic, steel and other commodities. Each terminal had its huge overhead cranes with traffic brought in and delivered by a sizeable fleet of articulated vehicles and flat-bed trailers. There were some large and important customers, including the Southampton shipping lines, the Steel Company of Wales, GKN, the Israeli Fruit Marketing Board and others.

Although I had run a cartage and terminals section in London, the new appointment proved there was much to be learned, particularly in terms of clients and their businesses. I absorbed the essentials quickly but got caught napping at a meeting of the South Wales group of the Institute of Transport, as it was then, when I was asked whether the Craig-y-Nos event would take place as usual. 'I shall be in touch about that,' was my ambiguous reply.

It turned out that my area hosted an annual event which had become extremely popular with important clients. Craig-y-Nos, I learned, was way out in one of the valleys off the Black Mountains and had semi-shrine status from being the country estate home of the once-famous diva Adelina Patti. There, apparently, we arranged each year to use the private theatre to stage small, intimate opera performances featuring the Neath Opera Group and principal singers of international renown. Happily, the Neath people always did most of the work, apart from sending invitations and paying bills. I thoughtlessly looked upon the first Craig-y-Nos event under my new leadership as just one more, albeit important, social function. But it proved so much more than that, in the most pleasant and memorable of ways.

Fenchurch Street station three days before Christmas 1960, and the carol singers from the Eastern Region Choral Society seem to be enjoying themselves, whatever the commuters thought about it.

The venue itself was a romantic and historic one. Madame Patti was a famous soprano who had made her European debut at Covent Garden in 1861. For the next twenty-five years her perfect voice and fine acting kept her in demand and she was held in high esteem. She purchased Craig-y-Nos in 1878 as a home and a retreat from her busy and extravagant lifestyle. The Neath & Brecon Railway had opened its steeply graded line past Craig-y-Nos in 1867 and subsequently built a station there with a private waiting room with elegant appointments for the diva's use. So revered and autocratic was Adelina Patti that both the Great Western Railway at Neath and the Midland Railway at Brecon kept private saloons available for her convenience. But back to my first encounter with the lady's home.

With the last container loaded, wagon twist-locks checked and the day's work at Swansea terminal all in order, the terminal manager Stan Judd and I set off for Craig-y-Nos, leaving the city in the late afternoon and emerging beyond the suburbs into the lonely area beyond. Much later than I expected our winding route revealed the architectural delight that was our destination. The opera performance was to be in two halves with the interval devoted to refreshments and social intercourse on the spacious balcony overlooking a dramatic valley panorama.

On this first occasion *The Marriage of Figaro* was performed and it was a delight, with the character of the house itself creating just the right ambience for the amazing music and Da Ponte's plot inviting full exploitation by the performers. By the time the next such event was held I was more relaxed; I knew my clients and my job much better and could respond more to the opera staging, this time of *La Bohème*. The modest size of the theatre made it an intimate event. One felt that the arias were being sung to you, almost as if you were there in the garret with the singers. The experience, enhanced by both the performance and the gracious surroundings, was indelible – one to be put on the opposite side of the coin to nights in a marshalling yard, disasters, disruptions and the various other tribulations that come with a railway career.

Music: Top of the Pops

BR could and did make a spectacular success of quite challenging publicity events. There was a very human side to one such occasion when Cedric Spiller took his daughter along.

In the 1980s, when InterCity had become a force to be reckoned with, a plan was hatched to undertake a non-stop, high-speed run from London Paddington to Bristol Temple Meads, timed to coincide *exactly* with the start and finish of the live BBC TV programme *Top of the Pops*. This feat required the most complex of arrangements involving civil engineers lifting line speeds at pinch points, mechanical engineers sorting out a specially shortened, spruced-up HST, special traffic staff clearing everyday stuff out of the way and, on top of this, accommodating two outside broadcast crews at Paddington and Bristol.

My part in this was minor. It was left to the InterCity managing director Cyril Bleasdale to mastermind the event with the help of public affairs and a host of operators. Needless to say, it was a precision operation. BR could do these things superbly when required to. Departure was spot on to the second and the arrival right on cue at Temple Meads with live television transmission was a brilliant achievement. The HST unit was named *Top of the Pops*, a pop group made a racket and the late, great Sir Jimmy Savile presided over the proceedings.

The point of this story is that I took my 15-year-old daughter on the train and on the way back to London at normal line speed she was chatting to Sir Jim when she said something that embarrassed me beyond belief. She asked for his autograph. Nothing happened. Jim sat there. A glare from me eventually made her realise that the word 'please' was quite important. 'Oh, yes,' said my daughter, 'please.' Then Jim signed. It was a wonderful piece of theatre from him that she has never forgotten. People say Jim was an enigma; no way, he was intelligent, kindness itself and extremely funny. Happy days!

Newsworthy

Mike Lamport joined the railway industry aiming to enter the public relations side of the business. His hopes of high interest and great variety in that field proved well founded.

Railway public relations officers had to present, instigate and quickly react to achieve a positive link between a much-maligned nationalised industry and a mostly sceptical media. To answer journalists' queries a twenty-four-hour on-call press service was maintained by the five regional press offices, as well as that of the British Railways Board. Photo opportunities and press conferences were frequently held to announce new initiatives and major changes. Another tool of the trade was to devise and manage 'facility trips' to positively highlight particular parts of the business to small groups of specialist journalists or, in some cases, individual writers.

However, not all such trips went according to plan or indeed produced the outcome that had been hoped for. In the 1970s, as public relations officer for BR's Newcastle Division, I invited the legendary Mike Amos – the 'John North' feature writer of the *Northern Echo* – to join me for a last ride on the soon-to-close Haltwhistle to Alston branch line. Let's just say that our wish to drown our sorrows with the locals at the loss of this lovely line ended with us being 'detained' in a pub and missing the last train of the night.

On another occasion, after an approach from a publisher who wanted to launch and test market a weekly railway partwork in the Tyne-Tees TV area, we agreed to host the winners of their Valentine's Day newspaper competition at Newcastle Central station. After the launch at the Station Hotel we invited the newspaper photographers to snap the happy couples – all of whom had first met either on a station or during a train journey – as they toasted each other with a glass of

Alston, where Mike Lamport was forced to stay overnight when a journalist facility trip overran. The branch DMU has just arrived from Haltwhistle, the junction with the Newcastle–Carlisle line. The branch closed in 1976, but trains are again run by the South Tynedale Railway. (Mike Lamport)

champagne on the 10.50 for King's Cross. All went well until my carelessly waved hand was taken to be the signal that we had finished and the train could start. To some incredulity, and a good deal of nervous laughter, the train slowly pulled away parting husband from wife and wife from husband, depending on which partner had been on the train and which on the platform for the photograph!

This story, of course, ended happily ever after, but not before some frantic telephone calls to the station staff at Darlington. The slightly tiddly, but reluctant travellers were asked to alight and remain there until a very embarrassed PR man (me) arrived on the following train to escort them back to an uproarious reunion with their spouses.

Even the dawn of the High Speed Train era was not without hitches. On one occasion, the large media party that I had eagerly encouraged to join me on the platform at Northallerton station, to record one of the first 125mph test runs, was instead hurried to a nearby pub to ease the pain of the wasted trip, and to hide my embarrassment. The much-heralded train had broken down south of York and failed to materialise!

On a happier note, the launch of the InterCity 125 trains on the East Coast Main Line was one of the highlights of my career. Working hand in hand with our marketing colleagues, we set out to create an exciting new brand and a buzz around these eye-catching trains under the tag line 'InterCity 125 – *the Journey Shrinker*'. The new trains themselves were a PR man's dream with their streamlined shape, striking yellow ends and oh-so-smooth ride; we used to impress guests by standing a threepenny bit on its edge on a table and then watching to see how long it remained upright as the train sped along. The 125 also had the unbeatable cachet of being able to 'cruise' at 125mph.

Despite having to follow the well-earned national acclaim that our counterparts on the Western Region had garnered two years previously when these magical trains had been first introduced, it was our job to create the excitement all over again. Our task was to 'sell' the new trains along the East Coast Main Line from London to Scotland, along with other destinations such as Middlesbrough, Hull and Cleethorpes. Succeed we did. But, when the interest we had created threatened to overcrowd the trains, and when reports of children travelling in the luggage stacks while their parents fought for standing room began to reach us, the marketing manager implored us to scale down our promotional activity. We had, in his words, been too successful. Not something you hear said many times in a PR career!

The passenger business apart, we also looked for innovative ways to promote freight. This ranged from events staged at sidings and collieries to the opening of new depots and facilities. On more than one occasion we, along with our media guests, travelled in passenger vehicles which we had requested be coupled to an air-braked freight service. Such unusual situations could mean making unusual arrangements, like the time when I had two dozen fish and chip suppers delivered to the passengers and crew of a freight train as it paused in Newcastle Central station on its regular overnight run from Teesside to the West of Scotland.

The image on the BR promotional postcard issued for the launch of Anglo-Scottish High Speed Train services on the East Coast Main Line in 1978. (Mike Lamport)

From time to time we enlisted TV personalities to help us get our message across. They included Sir Jimmy Savile, Barbara Windsor, Kathy Staff of *Last of the Summer Wine* fame and even Orville the Duck who, as the star of a summer show in Scarborough, was roped in to help promote the steam-hauled Scarborough Spa Express programme to holidaymakers and day trippers. On its inaugural run none other than No. 4472 *Flying Scotsman* hauled the train from York to Harrogate and Leeds before returning to York and on to Scarborough. On the initial stage of the journey I was thrilled to accompany a journalist to the cab of probably the most famous steam locomotive in the world – and by way of the corridor tender, the route of relief enginemen decades before. To emerge on to that hallowed footplate as we travelled over Arthington Viaduct and then through Bramhope Tunnel was a truly memorable experience.

Arriving at the BR Property Board (BRPB) in 1984 I quickly discovered that the business of the board broke down into three main categories: earning rental income from the BR estate; selling off surplus land – something that was actively encouraged by the government and was seen by some as 'selling the family silver'; and being custodians of BR's non-operational estate. Much of the latter was the legacy of the 'Beeching years' and included thousands of miles of disused trackbeds, along with hundreds of bridges, viaducts and tunnels.

The initial run of the Scarborough Spa Express behind No. 4472 Flying Scotsman *was followed by another steam-hauled special, this time to mark the reopening of the spa and hauled by No. 46229* Duchess of Hamilton, *seen here setting off with a good head of steam and a strong exhaust. (Mike Lamport)*

My door was soon being beaten down by a succession of eager young surveyors, all keen to enlist my help in advertising the availability of a seemingly endless supply of 'small business units', more commonly known as railway arches. Many of these were more Arthur Daley-like than the wine bars and health clubs they hoped to have renting their refurbished premises. However, the more I learnt about their plans and the more I saw for myself how, for fairly small levels of investment, a railway arch could be transformed into an attractive and flexible working space, the more I wanted to help them. Between us we devised the Festival of the Arches – a nationwide promotional programme of launch events whose twin aims were to raise the profile of the board as an investor and attract a new breed of higher-paying tenants to replace the car breakers of yore.

The festivals were launched in London, Manchester and Glasgow with the London-based premiere taking place in the cavernous arches beneath the platforms at Elephant & Castle station. Here, we built stages and exhibition stands to showcase the wares of our many and varied small tenants. They included an Italian pasta maker, an upmarket bathroom store and Cannons, a health club situated on the banks of the River Thames underneath Cannon Street station. While in Manchester we highlighted a ski slope under Victoria station and in Glasgow there was a hairdresser and a bed manufacturer.

As I had hoped, the 'underneath the arches' theme appealed to the media in the regions where we held the events and even the *Sunday Times Magazine*. The latter, under the headline 'Goodbye Arch Villains', featured their choice of stories from arch tenants, including an Aberdeen fishmonger, a London golf driving range and bus enthusiasts who used an arch in Huddersfield to restore veteran double-deckers!

As a railwayman first and foremost I was always on the lookout for opportunities to link the work of the Property Board with the big railway. For the 150th anniversary of the London & Greenwich – London's first railway, which was unique in that it was built entirely on arches – I found the perfect way to celebrate it and ensure that the name of the Property Board was seen by a wider audience. Over the August Bank Holiday we joined with Chris Green's newly created and promotion-friendly Network South East in taking over Cannon Street station which was normally closed at weekends. In it we not only staged a major model railway exhibition, with layouts covering a large area of the concourse, but we also managed to fill nearly all of the platforms with locomotives and rolling stock, including a particularly special General Utility Van, or GUV, which I used as an exhibition vehicle decked out with BRPB promotional material. The GUV was dressed externally with a large Property Board red and blue buildings silhouette logo which, despite my promise, I 'forgot' to remove before the van was put back into traffic the next day. What observers must have made of this unique, one-sided livery during the remaining period of the vehicle's life I do not know, but I recall seeing it in a parcels train at Wolverhampton some months later. As you can imagine I viewed it with a mixture of humour, pride and a little guilt!

An event and a new image devised to draw attention to railway arches as a potential business location. (Mike Lamport)

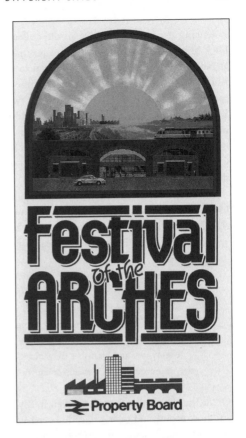

I later joined Network South East and during those days, and for some time after privatisation, I worked for the West Anglia and Great Northern train operating company, or WAGN as it became known. We, in common with all of the other new NSE divisions, had to suggest our own logo device. For the GN part this was relatively simple as the distinctive outline of Cubitt's arched frontage of King's Cross station readily leant itself to use; but what of West Anglia? This was a name that had been contrived a few years earlier when, thanks to the usual Treasury impositions, electrification spending priorities had had to be divided between Anglia East (to Norwich) and Anglia West (to Cambridge).

At the last minute a suitable image was found – a heron – and for the next few years the West Anglia route became known as the Heron Line. Anyone who knows the route from Liverpool Street to Cambridge via Bishop's Stortford will attest to the fact that there is usually one or more of these birds to be seen along the way. Indeed, when an artificial pond was created by BR engineers while creating a triangular junction at Stansted, a plastic model of a heron was planted at the centre of the island to mark the line's association with the bird and, hopefully, to help save the lives of the fish in the pond!

During my time at WAGN an old colleague came back into my life. This was Dick Shinkins, long retired from his position of divisional public relations officer at Norwich. He had been instrumental in ensuring that Benjamin Gimbert and Jimmy Nightall, two heroes of a wartime incident near Soham on the Ely to Ipswich line, were suitably honoured at a twin naming ceremony of two BR Rail Express Systems Class 47 locomotives, held in the nearby railway town of March in 1985. These locomotives apart, Dick was concerned that there were no proper memorials to Gimbert and Nightall who had, by their selfless action, saved the Cambridgeshire town of some 5,000 souls from untold death and destruction on that June night in 1944.

Working with the local Littleport Society and the Soham town council, Dick and I arranged for a large plaque to be fixed to the wall of the town's library building, right in the heart of this tight-knit Fenland community. The plaque was unveiled on 22 July 1992 by Ron Barber, a descendant of the Nightall family. It reads:

> To the Memory of James William Nightall G.C.
> A Son of Littleport and a Railwayman
> Locomotive fireman James Nightall was posthumously awarded the
> George Cross for his heroism in saving the people and town of Soham
> from death and destruction on the 2nd of June 1944. He died aged
> twenty two and his driver Benjamin Gimbert GC was badly injured as
> they removed a blazing wagon laden with bombs from an ammunition train.

Of all the words that I have written in my career, these are the ones of which I am most proud, and over a decade later I was honoured to be asked by the Royal British Legion to lay a wreath on behalf of railwaymen and women at a rededication ceremony at this memorial on Armistice Day 2004. In that same year Dick succeeded in his goal of seeing a similar memorial to Benjamin Gimbert erected in the centre of Soham and, to the sound of a Royal British Legion band, we proudly marched together through the streets. The preceding church service had featured Dick's specially written *Soham Hymn*, which was sung in memory of the Fenland railway heroes; it contains the following verse:

> Five thousand souls for food to you did crave;
> five thousand more saved from cruel grave
> in these, our Fens by railwaymen so brave.
> Alleluya, Alleluya!

European Night(mare) Services

In the late 1990s Theo Steel spent an interesting period working on the London & Continental bid for Eurostar and the Channel Tunnel Rail Link.

One of my main activities was trying to sort out the European Night Services (ENS) part of the L&CR, where the plan was to operate night seat-cum-sleeper trains from London to Amsterdam, or Dortmund/Frankfurt, and from Glasgow/Manchester and Swansea/Plymouth to Paris. A major issue for the Parliamentary Channel Tunnel Bill in the late 1980s was the provision of beyond-London services and the potential benefits to the regions. I recall that in the document for consultation we were told that the services should be provided to make a profit, not just because they were desirable – wise words in Bob Reid's introduction that somehow got lost along the way! Additionally, between the late 1980s and early 1990s the UK did not join the Schengen agreement, which allowed for journeys between European Union states to be passport-free. As a result, security became much more of a focus with a requirement for pre-journey checks.

Seven short Regional Eurostar trains (now in use in France) were built, and to complement them, 139 ENS vehicles were ordered for operation on the above routes in 1993. The fleet was ordered from Alsthom and the vehicles were assembled at the Met Cam works in Birmingham. The components were often specialist and widely sourced. The 139 vehicles consisted of twenty service vehicles, forty-eight seated vehicles and seventy-one sleepers. The plan was for the London services to operate in eight eight-car semi-fixed rakes – two to and from Amsterdam – with one spare. The beyond-London rakes would be seven-car sets made up of three seating, one service and three sleepers per rake, the London sets featuring four sleepers. Eight operating rakes and one spare were planned.

ENS was a joint venture between European Passenger Services, owning 58 per cent, and the German, French and Dutch railway systems (DB, SNCF and NS), with 14 per cent each. The Belgian network (SNCB) had an operating contract.

The prospect of serious problems was clear by 1996 with the rolling stock built late and the vehicles proving technically challenging, despite a great deal of effort from Alsthom and the project teams. I recall being told that each vehicle had 2km of wiring in it. Within the UK, pairs of Class 37 diesel electric locomotives were planned to haul the trains over the non-electrified routes, with a generator van converted from a redundant Mark III sleeper to supplement power. Class 92 electrics would be used through the Channel Tunnel and on electrified routes. The trains would be hauled by various locomotives on the Continent and were to be assisted by banking locomotives in the Ardennes. Conventional railways would be used throughout, although the vehicles were capable of 200km/h.

Implementing such challenging plans may have been an operator's dream, but to the bean counters it was a nightmare – particularly as the overnight rail market was evaporating all over Europe and, more particularly, yields were being challenged by the emergence of low-cost airlines. At the time, we could not foresee that fifteen years on, Eurostar journeys would not yet have exceeded 10 million, far short of the 15 million predicted.

The beyond-London services had the most challenging bottom line and in late 1996 various route options were looked at; Switzerland and southern France among them. However, SNCF were not keen to accept further night trains. In a parallel search for more viable options, we investigated alternative vehicle uses for at least the seater vehicles, but they were low capacity, heavy and unproven operationally.

While all this was going on, construction was advancing. A train of sixteen vehicles was tested over Shap Summit with a Class 92 at the head, breasting the bank at 55mph, although to my eternal regret I was not on the train. This test revealed that a lot of the specifications were not being matched, so the fitting out of the sleepers was halted after about thirty-five vehicles were completed.

The contract for the vehicles included a performance bond. After almost a year of discussions we had no alternative but to activate this in December 1997. The result was a trip to Paris in late January 1998 where the situation was summed up by the then chairman of Alsthom, who said: 'We can't build the vehicles and you don't want them so let's cut our losses.' After a year of posturing, the deal was sorted in ten minutes. A financial arrangement emerged broadly on a fifty-fifty basis between builder and potential operator. There was then the complicated task of splitting the liabilities and unwinding the vehicle leases.

By June 1998 the ENS company had become dormant, ending the dream of wide-ranging night services to and from Europe. I left L&CR for First Great Eastern after two years of very interesting experiences. As for the vehicles, they were ultimately sold to VIA Canada who used them on day trains out of Montreal and on the 'Ocean' between Montreal and Halifax. Some of the sleeper shells are fitted out as diners or baggage vans. VIA bought the equipment for £29 million and then spent a lot more money making them compliant. They ride beautifully from my limited sampling.

A lot of effort went into the ENS project and it was some time before the train paths in the United Kingdom were abandoned. And the Class 92 locomotives are still under-utilised. Perhaps the High Speed 2 rail link to the Midlands and North will eventually lead to passenger services originating beyond London, but I doubt there will ever be sleeper services. One calculation we did showed that to be profitable we needed an average yield of £500 for a single trip between London and Frankfurt in a single-berth sleeper!

To Pull or Not to Pull

That was the question for Jim Dorward as he headed from Euston to Glasgow via the West Coast Main Line.

On Friday 13 April 1979 – not a good omen – I had to travel from London to Bonnie Dundee, my home town. As a result of the catastrophic collapse of Penmanshiel Tunnel on 17 March, causing the tragic death of two contractors working there, the East Coast Main Line was closed between Berwick-upon-Tweed and Dunbar. To avoid the replacement bus service, I had decided to travel via the West Coast Main Line on the 09.45 from Euston to Glasgow Central.

The journey was uneventful until approaching Motherwell, where the train was not booked to call. We were stopped at the signal protecting Motherwell's main Down platform. After several minutes I looked out and was surprised to see the guard in the cess speaking to the driver of the Class 87 locomotive. They seemed to be having a long conversation, usually not a good sign, I thought, and probably the guard thought also, that we were going to be stationary for some time. When the conversation ended, he started to move back along the train but did not climb aboard. As he walked, the signal cleared to a proceed aspect. The driver seemed to be in a hurry and was quickly on the move. We were on a falling gradient and fast gathering speed. It was clear that we were off to Glasgow in a 'driver only' mode.

Do I pull the communication cord, I thought? A quick assessment was needed. If I pull the cord we will no doubt stop in the vicinity of Lesmahagow Junction and have to sit there for some time; not a good outcome, I concluded, given the number of trains that use the junction. If I don't pull the cord, the train will complete its journey within the next fifteen minutes and the likelihood of the guard's services being required during that time is probably very small. I decided, on balance, not to pull the cord.

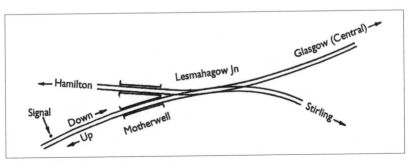

Lesmahagow Junction, where Jim Dorward had an unexpected delay.

Bereft of his train, the poor guard must have immediately reported his unfortunate separation to the signalman in Motherwell box. It would appear that the signalman took the view that he could not have a train proceeding without a guard and so, with our speed now up to 60mph, there was a sudden and severe brake application. I began to wonder about the wisdom of my decision. We ground to a halt some considerable distance beyond Lesmahagow Junction and, surprise, surprise, we sat there for at least thirty minutes until the guard arrived. My fellow passengers and I on that busy Good Friday train were forty minutes late into Glasgow Central, and some other trains had also been delayed. Yet we had completed the journey with the proper establishment on board. But to this day I am not sure if I made the right decision.

A Near Thing

David Crathorn's plan to spend a day clearing his paperwork did not quite work out that way.

In May 1965, as the stationmaster at Cricklewood, I decided to catch up on some paperwork. Even though it was Bank Holiday Monday, I went into the office, lit the gas fire (which the early turn porter would normally have done) and was soon up to my elbows in forms and reports. The early turn booking clerk, Eddie, came in with a cup of tea and after only two or three sips the telephone rang. It was the signalman in Cricklewood Junction signal box asking for the stationmaster to go to the box. Now this was a busy, highly graded signal box, usually staffed by two special category signalmen and a box 'boy'. But, by tradition, on Bank Holidays only one signalman was rostered. The fact that on such days there were many special workings does not appear to have ever been taken into account.

When I went into the box, the signalman quietly explained his problem. He had been offered a diesel multiple unit bound for Bedford down the Fast Line and had pulled off his signals, which had automatically pulled off the Down Fast Distant slot at Watling Street. No sooner had he done this than he realised he ought to have 'turned' the DMU on to the Down Slow at Cricklewood, to clear the Fast Line for a following Down special express.

Disconcerted by his error in priorities, the signalman had quickly thrown his levers back in the frame causing the signals to go to danger. Thinking that the DMU could not have sighted the clear signals, he made his big mistake. The junction was now free and he changed the crossover points and pulled off Fast to Slow to permit the DMU to be overtaken by the express.

There was an immediate diesel unit horn and, to his horror, the signalman saw that the unit was following his original intention and rounding the bend towards him at what seemed like the normal higher speed for the Fast Line. In fact, the driver had managed to slow down somewhat but still went through the 25mph crossover at 40mph, finally stopping halfway to Brent Junction No. 1 signal box. Fortunately, there was no derailment.

The DMU driver had walked purposefully to the signal box to have 'words' with the signalman before returning to his cab and driving on. The latter, chastened somewhat, had then requested the stationmaster to stay with him until the end of his shift at 2 p.m. There were no more problems that day.

Survey Surprises

On-train passenger surveys were vital but extremely wearing on voice, feet and temperament. They also produced some surprises, as Peter Spedding recalls.

The 1960s was a time of many developments and the LMR passenger train business needed better information about its customers. It was decided to use on-train questionnaires, and management trainees currently in training, who would benefit from the experience, were selected for the job. The first exercise was to last two weeks on the Midland lines in January 1965.

We operated in teams of three, handing each passenger a questionnaire during the journey and collecting the completed ones later. It contained a variety of pertinent questions and the whole exercise was quite intense. We usually had to hurry round from one booked train to the next.

On one particular day I boarded an afternoon train at St Pancras with my two colleagues and immediately set off along the corridor to distribute my questionnaires. With many stops and a great deal of passenger interchange there was no time to lose. One of the compartments in a first-class coach had the blinds drawn and a door reservation label in the name of the area manager at St Pancras. I knocked, entered and proffered the questionnaires to the two occupants: an older man of about 60 and a younger one of around 45. The older man got very angry and expressed his views about the intrusion forcibly. In this day and age it would probably have amounted to verbal abuse. Explanation proving to no avail, I retreated.

A little later in the journey I was passing through the restaurant car when the younger man approached me. He explained that the older man was a circuit judge on his way to a provincial town. I could then understand that a judge would have to avoid potentially prejudicial contacts, and although no direct apology was given, I did at least get an offer to complete the questionnaire.

Another survey occasion involved the useful 00.05 train from St Pancras to Leeds. On the night of Sir Winston Churchill's funeral the train was full of Yorkshire ladies travelling home after lining the streets of London to pay their respects. At that time of night it needed some determination to go through the train to hand out questionnaires and even more to collect them. The team planned to distribute the forms as soon as the train left St Pancras and then collect those left on seats at the end of the journey. I opened one compartment door to find a young couple lying along the seat doing what young couples do. Rather at a loss for words I asked for completion of the form. Unfazed, the man replied, 'Yes, just leave it on the seat.' This I did and withdrew in some confusion. Collecting the questionnaires later I looked with interest to see what the young couple had written, and saw: Station From: *St Pancras*. Station To: *Bedford*. Purpose of Journey: *Pleasure!!!!* The exclamation marks made the occasion especially memorable.

'Something of a Luxury'

This was one view of area managers, as expressed to Dennis Simmonds, but his experiences at Portsmouth proved very much the opposite.

As in most large organisations, old loyalties and prejudices often lingered, and the Southern Region proved no exception. As a former London Midland man arriving via the Western, I got a whiff of this when appointed as area manager at Portsmouth. At my interview the divisional manager had made no bones about his views on area managers, telling me that he regarded them as 'something of a luxury'. The 'welcome' continued on finding that no office had been provided for me. I was to sit on the sofa in the office of the Portsmouth station manager, himself a lifetime South Western man comfortably ensconced behind a half-acre desk. Happily, contact with the local shipping manager, Len Wheeler, secured me a base in his assistant's vacant office.

Shortly after my arrival I arranged to meet the lord mayor, but got only complaints about BR for my pains. Fortunately, he retired the following month and the new incumbent, Major Dennis Darling Connors, proved much more co-operative and was most enthusiastic about my suggestions for a programme of Portsmouth events weekends, which would include rail travel. I was given a lesson in local politics when this plan foundered, all because the boarding house owned by the incumbent chairman of the hoteliers association would not have benefited.

A few weeks later another initiative met with more success. I was invited to go on board the USS *Springfield* which was on a courtesy visit to Portsmouth. There I learned that a third of the crew had gone to London on a day trip paid for by the Admiralty. Fine, but they had travelled by coach. The lord mayor's secretary helped me to track down the dockyard maintenance commander who decided such matters, and along with my passenger representative we secured the business to rail.

We simply had to reserve the rear four coaches of a twelve-car London train for the party, which would involve no extra costs other than the price of the window labels. As many of these vessels were 'dry', the on-train bar made a handsome profit, too.

At Haslemere, the Down side goods yard had been closed, the tracks lifted, and car parking provided on the roadways. Even so, there was a waiting list of over 200 names for annual parking tickets. Clearly something needed to be done to provide more space. Accordingly, I arranged for the area civil engineer to let me have twenty wagons of spent ballast and then paid the local coal merchant to use his grab and tipper lorry to distribute the material along the unsurfaced area. The stationmaster provided some staff to rake the ballast level on the following Sunday and, once motorists had used it enough to consolidate it, we were able to issue eighty new car-parking tickets.

Some experiences are quite unsettling, like the time when I was riding in the cab of an express train booked to run non-stop from Woking to Waterloo. I was on my way to a meeting at Wimbledon, and when the platform starter there showed red I told the driver that I would drop off if we had to stop. When the aspect then changed to a single yellow and the driver accelerated, I abandoned my plan to alight and returned to the driving cab, in time to see that we were passing the next signal at red. I shouted at the driver to stop and at first he responded and brought the train to a stand, but then started off again because he saw a green ahead. My insistence that he should stop again and speak to the signalman was rejected and on he went to Clapham Junction where we were halted by signals.

The consequences of this event could have been serious as it transpired that we had run through a pair of trailing points and narrowly missed an empty stock train being put into Durnsford Road Sidings. I had accompanied the driver on to Waterloo and had him relieved there, but the eventual joint inquiry was an unsatisfactory affair because the driver maintained that I had actually instructed him to proceed. I had tried to avoid exaggerating his offence in my evidence but, with hindsight, this was a mistake; a human one, perhaps, but in the primary interest of safety I should have presented the offence more bluntly.

A couple of months after the Wimbledon episode I was again in a driving cab, this time returning from a meeting, when another incident occurred which showed that things can still go wrong even when the intentions are good. After I left the train at Portsmouth & Southsea High Level there was a complete power failure as it continued on towards Portsmouth Harbour. The driver had reason to believe an on-train fault had occurred and decided to let his train freewheel into the terminal in order to clear the main line. At the time the new panel signal box had been introduced, but the re-signalling had not included the points at Portsmouth Harbour because they were in good order. Unfortunately, these were wind-over points and not slap-over ones and they had failed in the half-open position. Result: the train dropped on to two tracks.

If there was one attribute required of an area manager it was the ability to apply common sense to a great variety of out-of-the-ordinary situations. This was exemplified one day when I was informed that, in flagrant disregard of instructions, a local freight train had gone into the exchange sidings of the Longmoor Military Railway at Liss to enable the locomotive to run round its train. Unfortunately, the locomotive had been derailed. When I got to the site shortly after the arrival of the breakdown gang, I found that they had put re-railing plates against its wheels, passed a chain around the adjacent sidings in order to anchor it, and were operating the crank in the chain to draw the locomotive up the plates and back on to the track – or so the gang foreman advised me. I had to point out that what was actually happening was that the adjacent siding, which was bedded in ash ballast, was being moved towards the locomotive and not the other way round!

Perhaps area managers were not just a luxury after all!

We Couldn't Keep Up

Writing of a banking locomotive incident, Bryan Stone observed that railway 'bankers never got a bonus, but they often kept the show on the road'.

By 1964 the steam to diesel transition was in full swing. The diesels didn't always realise their promise, but the steam locomotives were reaching the end of a long and often hard life. The interface was difficult, and shifting. A priceless experience befell me on 9 April 1964, near Scunthorpe. I suppose such things happened elsewhere; indeed, there is a description in D.L. Smith's *Tales of the Glasgow & South Western Railway* of the Stranraer Harbour pilot finding himself in a similar predicament.

I was in the Doncaster divisional office at the time and I was sent out to report on some of the Scunthorpe area workings, also in flux before the steam shed closed. So it was that I was on No. 63793, a Class O4/8 steam locomotive, rolling light engine down the 1 in 100 gradient from Scunthorpe to Gunhouse Junction. We were the Gunhouse banker, assisting heavy freights of coal, coke and iron ore on the ex-Great Central line alongside the canal from Thorne. At Keadby, after the bridge over the Trent, with its redundant three-position semaphore signals, the line dropped to Gunhouse Junction near the river bank and then took off at 1 in 100 on to the Wolds at Scunthorpe. There were a lot of trains and most, exceeding a defined single load, took assistance. The banker stood in a spur at 'Gunness' and waited for the call to action.

A load of ironstone headed by a Brush Type 2 diesel – Class 31 today – rolled off the bridge and stopped. The twenty-two iron ore wagons were over a single load, so No. 63793 drew out and buffered up, but was not coupled, to the brake van. We hung out our tail lamp while the guard withdrew his, and there was a hoot from the diesel as the Gunhouse starter was pulled off. We whistled back and the regulator

Showing its age but still game, Gunhouse Junction banker No. 63793 stands at Scunthorpe. (Bryan Stone)

was opened. No. 63793 started to 'woof' satisfyingly. This, too, was a steam/diesel interface and getting both to start smoothly together was not easy. At this point it was always interesting to see how many wagons were indeed being pushed – buffers compressed, couplings slack – as opposed to being pulled by the train engine.

No. 63793 was one of many O4s to receive a 1940s Thompson 100A boiler. Below the belt, however, she was as built in 1918 for the army, strong as an ox, with no automatic brakes and nearly fifty years old. These old O4s, though strong, were notoriously slow. A steady plod was usual. The Brush diesel ahead, weak on starting, was happier at a higher speed, and once into a suitable power range took the bit firmly. A gap opened up between 63793 and the brake van and we couldn't catch up. The guard mockingly waved goodbye from his receding brake van. Of course, he might still have 'stuck' so we had to watch out, but after 2 miles the iron ore train was well over the top and away through Scunthorpe station. We drew forlornly to a stand at the station signal box. There, an amused signalman, who knew what had happened and had not been panicked into sending the 'train divided' bell signal, saw our tail lamp and gave Gunhouse the 2-1 'out of section' signal.

Veteran 63793 struggled on at Frodingham shed until May 1965, but with progressive dieselisation fewer trains took the Gunhouse banker. By our showing, you couldn't blame them, but if you got an Austerity locomotive in the role, it worked rather better.

The Down Postal

How an innocent conversation with a postman came to haunt Peter Spedding.

In 1963, when working as a relief clerk in the freight rolling stock and freight operating sections of the general manager's office at Euston House, I lived in a house close to Berkhamsted station on the West Coast Main Line. In the June of that year, when the light of day was long enough to make it worthwhile, I decided to walk to the pick-up point on the Down Fast Line north of the station to see the 20.30 Post Office train ex Euston pick up the mailbags on the move at about 21.05.

On my arrival the postman was already attaching the two mail pouches to the apparatus and securing them to the standard with string. He explained that this was to prevent the draught of the passing train drawing the bags into the side. The train duly passed at speed with the lights along the sides of the vehicles illuminated, and with a double bang swept the two pouches into the extended net. With the excitement over, the postman, whose day was now finished, and I went for a pint and discussed all manner of things about the Post Office and how the postal services operated. We parted the best of friends and went our separate ways.

On 7 August the Great Train Robbery took place between Leighton Buzzard and Cheddington, only about 10 miles from my pleasant and seemingly innocent

Postal trains no longer operate over British main lines but preservation has embraced that once-important activity, as demonstrated by this Great Western Society set on a visit to Wansford in 2004.

conversation with the postman. The robbery was headline news; every avenue of enquiry was being rigorously pursued. As a result, I spent several days in fear and trembling at the thought of the postman denouncing me to the authorities as the man who had been quizzing him on how the railway side of the operation fitted together!

Perhaps fortunately, I never saw him again.

Joint Line Adventures

The Great Northern & Great Eastern Joint Line from Doncaster to March had a special character of its own, as Bryan Stone's notebooks help to recapture.

Where would you look for Park Drain, Potterhanworth and Pinchbeck? And what about the 'two for the price of one' stations at Haxey & Epworth, Branston & Heighington, Nocton & Dunston, Blankney & Metheringham, Scopwick & Timberland and French Drove & Gedney Hill? Down the Joint Line, of course; a railway which, in its own way, epitomised John Betjeman's reference, in his 'Lincolnshire Tale' to 'down a long lane in the county of Lincs'. These stations were mostly down a long lane, for the Joint Line ran through some quite remote areas. When we mentioned the Joint Line in Doncaster, we always meant the Great Northern & Great Eastern Joint Line south to Whitemoor. There were others around our patch – the South Yorkshire, the Axholme, the GN&LNW from Bottesford, the M&GN – but this was the Joint Line as we knew it.

It was a 92-mile-long railway starting 3 miles south of Doncaster at Black Carr. It ran across open country to meet the Great Central route at Gainsborough and then south-east over the only hill to Pyewipe Junction. There, the Lancashire, Derbyshire & East Coast line joined from Langwith and a second-rate marshalling yard used to provide traffic for onward loads. After Pyewipe an avoiding line passed south around the city of Lincoln and its high cathedral to continue into the fen country to Sleaford, with its junctions for Boston, Grantham and Nottingham, and another curious avoiding line. Spalding, too, had a complicated rail layout to link its three routes and six directions – the Joint Line itself, the Peterborough to Grimsby line and the M&GN's east–west route. The few gentle gradients of earlier sections were now replaced by a line heading straight and near level, on over Murrow's flat crossing with the M&GN, and so to Whitemoor and March.

It was a late creation. The Great Northern Railway in the 1870s and '80s was established in the Yorkshire and Nottinghamshire coalfields and used its main line as the outlet to the south. That was not a good outlook for the rural Great Eastern Railway, especially when coal traffic took off and passenger demands increased. The GER wanted to tap the coalfields by building northwards, a serious threat to the

On the GN&GE Joint Line, the Sleaford level crossing gates have been closed and the 'board' is off for the English Electric Type 4 diesel and its Up express passenger train. (Bryan Stone)

GNR near-monopoly. What emerged was this joint line, using sections already built, one or two cut-offs, and with a new Spalding–March section. All were put into a GN&GE Joint Line holding and operated as one railway. The coal was shared, easing pressures on the East Coast Main Line by reaching London via Cambridge. The LDEC at Pyewipe, and GC traffic via Gainsborough, added to the strategic opportunity. Whitemoor became the LNER's biggest hump-shunting yard, semi-automated from the 1930s, and there were once 7,000 coal wagons and empties passing through every day.

On an average weekday the Freight Working Timetable for the Joint Line recorded, with various qualifications, some sixty-five to seventy northbound freights from Whitemoor, two-thirds of them mineral empties. Some turned off at Sleaford for Colwick, or Lincoln for Langwith, the rest reaching Doncaster. The Up road was similar, with some forty coal block trains going south every day. Many ran in the night, one behind the other, seldom in the right order, some with Austerities and Class 9Fs, some behind diesels.

The Joint Line was virtually flat. The ruling grade for loaded Up trains was 1 in 400, and for Down, mainly empties, 1 in 200. But such was the level of use, and calculating from the Working Timetable, there were some seventy signal boxes between March and Black Carr, some switched out at night. The traffic only paused on Sunday afternoon. There were also countless level crossings, each with gates and some with signals. The line speed was 60mph, though junctions and crossings, shoe-horned into existing layouts, were often lower. At night, in the total darkness, you could see signals a long way off, and the view of Lincoln Cathedral from around Potterhanworth was an engineman's privilege.

Passenger trains were few, those stations with euphonious names being closed in 1959–61, leaving the displaced users to go to the Lincolnshire Road Car Company, with whom we maintained careful relations. Of three through trains a day, one was the North Country Continental, Harwich–Liverpool, connecting with the night service from Hook of Holland. It branched off at Gainsborough for Sheffield. Once run with 4-6-0 Sandringham Class engines, by 1963/64, after a period with Britannias, it was the prerogative of 1,750hp diesels. The other two through trains were Colchester–Newcastle and Lowestoft–York, both substantial trains with buffet cars.

After the Doncaster and Lincoln districts had merged – to the fury of the Lincoln people – I sometimes took a 05.55 Doncaster to Lincoln train, did my work and came back on the York or the Newcastle. One day in spring 1964, called to March, I joined D6748's crew at Doncaster to ride with them into the darkness. At Lincoln, this became a parcels train, made up to 400 tons. I was enjoying this until, to quote again Betjeman's Lincolnshire poem: 'All of a sudden the pony fell dead.' D6748 went very quiet, and near Digby we rolled to a standstill. My driver friend identified the overspeed governor as the cause of the trouble. Once reset, and starting carefully, it held for the rest of the ride, now of course rather delayed.

Well, troubles never come singly. After a long day I went to join the crew on D356, a 2,000hp engine, on 4S08; it was the 20.35 Whitemoor–Millerhill fast freight, first stop Doncaster Decoy at 23.11. 'A heavy train of 48 wagons, equal to 53,' said the guard. We left, by my notebook, at 21.12 and our driver started to make up time, but alas, not for long. Entering Spalding we crossed the River Welland, on its way to the Wash. Approaching Welland Bridge signal box, at low speed and under clear signals, we were suddenly hurled forward against the panel by an abrupt stop. D356 shut down, and the driver recovered and said, 'Look, no vacuum.' It was pitch black. The guard got down with his oil hand lamp and walked forward, examining the train. The second man went to the signal box. We were inside fixed signals, restored to danger both ways because we might have been off the road, blocking tracks. The train was in fact on the rails, but divided by a broken coupling. The torn brake pipe had applied the vacuum brake hard, and the rear portion of the train had buffered up. The engine had stopped quickest!

An 'instanter' coupling, today forgotten but then in widespread use, had failed. This was a three-link loose coupling but with the middle link pear-shaped so that when turned through 90 degrees it made a shorter coupling. It was a cheap and easy way of holding a fast train together without slack and was much used on the Great Western Railway. Unfortunately, being like a standard three-link coupling, forged in the workshop by hand from a heated steel bar, bent to a loop and hammered on an anvil to make a joint, its quality was never sure. No one could test the joint and broken couplings were a regular risk.

Thirty-two minutes later we were coupled up again but downgraded because the wagons behind the broken brake pipe were now unbraked. We became Class 6, required to run more slowly, and lost our priority. It was a leisurely trip to Doncaster and we eventually arrived at 01.23, 132 minutes late. Not the least result of this

On a typical long, straight, lonely stretch of the Joint Line near Digby, D6748 has failed with a heavy Doncaster to March parcels train. (Bryan Stone)

incident was the disruption it caused, for in 1964 on a weekday in the two hours from 19.45 to 21.50, ten Class 4 trains ran north from the busy Whitemoor Down yard. Among them, in addition to our 4S08, were three Whitemoor to Edinburgh Millerhill express freights.

There were very few passenger trains on the route. In 1966 I was running staff seminars in Lincoln on customer service, going the extra mile, a soft answer turning away wrath, etc. Most of those attending were double my age and experience. On 7 January I went early, ran my session and was relaxing on the way home on the 11.30, the Newcastle, engine D5546. At Kesteven the brakes went on and all went quiet. A contact breaker on the engine had opened, I heard later. It was reset, and ten minutes after that we were rolling again.

At Lea, before Gainsborough, it opened again. This time a fire broke out in the switchboard cabinet, and although quickly extinguished, a cheerful guard said that we were here to stay. He knew about my seminars so he asked me for help with the passengers. There was no escape, so we went through that train, mercifully quiet in this first week of January, and asked about journeys and connections. It was hair-raising! They were going all over the north and to Scotland, and were mostly sceptical about our ability to achieve anything. We could only promise to send details forward – no mobile phones then – and at least organise free tea and coffee at the buffet. In due course, under the appropriate rules, a 2,750hp diesel arrived from Lincoln and propelled us to Gainsborough. My notes, for Doncaster Control, were deposited with the signalman. Then, with the fresh engine now in front, we set off again to Doncaster, sixty-eight minutes late.

BR junior managers were rostered 'on call'. You had to stay near your telephone and arrange cover in an emergency. That phone would ring at 2 a.m. 'Hello. Oh, it's you, inspector. Where are you? What's the trouble?' 'Down the Joint Line,' seemed a frequent answer. Out would come the story: run-through crossing gates or, more critically, off the road. 'How does it look?'

There was more, but that was the critical enquiry, because the inspector, with far more experience than I, didn't want me under his feet. If the incident was serious, with deaths, injuries, police etc., I would have to go. 'They're doing well; we'll get squared up alright.'

'Fine, but call if you need me.'

The following morning we would meet and sort out a report. Sometimes it was a serious matter. Mineral wagons were mostly 16-ton four-wheelers, some of them still of wood, all with plain oil bearings, loose-coupled and with no continuous brakes. Divided trains, with broken springs, were legion and could easily end up in a wreck. I always felt there must be countless bits of mineral wagons along the lonelier sections of the Joint Line. Clearing the line to get traffic moving would often mean pushing wagons over the embankment into the fen, to be picked up at leisure.

If I had to turn out, it could be a long job. Driving at dead of night you could end up on narrow lanes, along the dykes, clutching the Ordnance Survey map until you saw lights in the distance to home in on. And yes, sometimes people were killed, like the five youngsters who stalled a worn-out car on Beckingham crossing in early 1968. The car ended up underneath the leading bogie of a 120-ton, 2,000hp diesel some 400yd further on. You never forget!

We also had many wrecks of our own, but they didn't usually get into the newspapers. One reason for the incidents was the new diesels. With them two things came together: sustained running at higher speeds, which greatly increased our mineral wagons' vulnerability to hot axle boxes, and all those closed stations and signal boxes switched out at night. These were incredibly lonely places. If no one heard that penetrating squeal or spotted the flame before the red-hot journal end fractured, then a wreck was inevitable. Coal was declining by then, but the Joint Line still came to a stand on such nights.

Other times were more lively. The Joint Line was a diversionary route when the East Coast Main Line was in trouble. In those days we also had the Grantham–Lincoln branch, which was kept at RA9 route availability for the biggest engines to run over it in emergency. This they did quite often, livening up the rural tenor of life at quiet places like Caythorpe and Harmston. I last saw an A1 Pacific go down there in October 1964.

There were some busy days in summer. I had become passenger manager at Doncaster and on summer Saturdays the Joint Line came to life. On 8 August 1964 I went to Skegness to add some encouragement to the local people in dealing with the huge influx of holidaymakers. They were very surprised; they never saw anyone from 'up there', they said. A mug of tea and I was in. Eighteen 'seasonals' came in that day, as well as twelve regular trains. Each seasonal had up to twelve coaches, usually on a tight turnaround and needing cleaning and servicing before their return working. All but four brought steam engines, mostly B1s, and went home with them again. It was, briefly, bedlam. These summer-only services came from Nottingham, Bradford, York, Leeds, Sheffield, Manchester and Birmingham, and more than eight of the eighteen would have taken the Joint Line from Doncaster to Lincoln and the 'new line' through Tumby Woodside.

That afternoon from Skegness I rode wearily back to Doncaster on No. 61388 on the Leeds train. The Saturday timetable from March to Doncaster also included some ten additional expresses, from Yarmouth and Lowestoft, Ely and Cambridge heading to the north. In the following years all this summer Saturday business fell away as habits changed and coaching stock for seasonals was drastically reduced, but it was an exciting time while it lasted. Timekeeping was liberal on such days. Crowds were unpredictable, steam engines needed water (61388 stopped on the Lincoln avoiding line for water, as the driver didn't know where there was any more), countless things went wrong and were sorted out. But the crowds were cheerful.

Now it has all gone: Whitemoor is a Network Rail engineering stores yard; the track is lifted to Spalding, north of Firsby and east of Lincoln; the coal has gone; other sunnier beach resorts are reached by low-cost airlines. Trains still go to Skegness, which is, I believe, just as bracing. Lincoln still has a direct London express, but via Newark, and the Joint Line we knew is today a near-forgotten name.

The Chief Clerk

It used to take a long time to become a chief goods or booking clerk. Many then never moved from their position and some became real characters, as Bill Robinson illustrates.

The clock gently ticked on the booking office wall. It clicked and moved to 08.15. Faint sounds could be heard of the last parcels being sheeted out for delivery that day. A trickle of passengers queued to buy their tickets for the 08.25 to Hull. The date stamping of the tickets and chink of the money going into the cash drawer confirmed that everything was quiet and in order.

The clock clicked to 08.18 and the arrival of the 08.05 from Hull could be heard from the office. Suddenly the door flew open. 'Whah! Morning all!' Joe, the chief clerk, had arrived. He took off his coat, donned a brown dust coat and sat behind his desk. A prolonged bout of coughing shattered the peace of the office. Once recovered, Joe rolled his first cigarette of the day and had another good cough.

Occasionally, after the early turn booking clerk had put a metal sheet up the chimney of the open fire to fill the office with smoke just before Joe's arrival, the coughing would be even worse. 'Whah! What's wrong?' Joe would ask.

'Don't know, wind must be in the wrong direction,' replied the far-from-innocent booking clerk.

The clock ticked and moved to 09.15. Joe was on his second cigarette and third bout of coughing. His expected visitor arrived, a bus conductor from East Yorkshire Motor Services. The bus company had a night safe in the booking office wall into which all the local conductors deposited their takings. Joe would count the contents of all the bags of cash and the conductor would indicate his agreement with the total. Some £200 was involved, most of it in copper and silver, hence Joe's coat at the front was shiny black to match his hands. As the clock clicked to eleven o'clock a taxi arrived to take Joe and the cash to the bank in town. The booking office resumed its quiet and orderly existence.

On his return, the chief clerk put on his dust coat again and set about having some food. Sometimes this would be fish and chips – out of the paper, of course. The whole event was worthy of a music hall act. Eggs were another choice, sometimes boiled in a little pan on the gas ring in the hearth of the open fire.

'Are my eggs done?' he would ask.

'No, not yet,' came the reply, followed shortly afterwards by a loud crack as the eggs exploded across the room. 'Whah! Was that my eggs?' Joe would exclaim plaintively.

Joe's poached eggs were a feast to behold. They were cooked in the same pan and Joe would toast the bread in front of the open fire. The completed dish was placed on his shiny black desk without a plate. Inevitably, the yolk would break and run on to the desktop. With a flourish Joe would sweep up the egg with the remaining toast and finish off the meal with relish. The end of his meal break was always marked by Joe getting up to use the telephone to call his wife. 'Hello Evie, any calls?' All that could be heard were a few squeaks, then 'any mail?' Further squeaks were followed by, 'we aren't having them!' With no further comment the call would be finished and the chief clerk resumed his duties.

The clock quietly marked the passing of the afternoon as Joe devoted himself to the office accounts and correspondence, interspersed with further cigarettes and bouts of coughing. Five o'clock came and the brown dust coat was hung up. The chief clerk's day was finished and he left to catch the next train to Hull. The clock ticked, the booking office was quiet and in order.

Are You Sure It Will Work?

For years, bullhead track in 60ft lengths was the standard for running lines, but now that was changing. Jim Dorward witnesses this at Barry Links in 1961.

It is a cold, foggy Sunday in January 1961 and I am at Barry Links on the East Coast Main Line between Monifieth and Carnoustie. Today's Sunday engineering job is special, so much so that the assistant district engineer is there in person. For the first time, the Perth district is about to offload long welded rails from a special train to be used on its first stretch of CWR – the continuous welded rail used to create track without fishplate joints. Barry Links is one of the district's 'race tracks'. It is on the level and dead straight between West Ferry (Dundee) and Elliot Junction (near Arbroath), making it an ideal location for this ultra-modern design of track, especially as the ballast conditions are excellent.

The engineering 'possession' of the line has been taken, the single-line working is in operation and the long welded rail train, with its rear brake van detached, has been hauled by a Dundee Class B1 steam locomotive into the first unloading position.

The train has several pairs of 420ft-long, flat-bottomed rails on board. It is subject to severe speed restriction as it, too, is revolutionary since the rails bend every time the train negotiates curved track. The chief mechanical and electrical engineer's people have had to figure out how the wagons can cope with this. We all had fears that the long rail sections would exert forces that would try to pull the wagons sideways off the track as the train moved over the tight reverse curves at each end of Dock Street Tunnel in Dundee, on its way to Barry Links.

The critical unloading moment has now come. Everyone watches with apprehension as the first pair of rails is anchored to the track. The permanent way inspector tells the guard to move the train forward at less than walking pace. The guard says, 'Are you sure it will work?' He is mildly reassured, the B1 effortlessly opens up, the chains tighten and then hold the two long rails stationary as the train starts to move. Off the end of the train they come, sliding slowly down the chutes to where they are wanted, and the collective tension eases.

The unloading operation continues without a hitch, the last two rails come off the train and sit exactly where we wanted them. The PWI breathes a sigh of relief, but then starts to worry about the next Sunday's challenge: the actual installation of the rails. This will require new skills. Not only have these long rails to be site-welded into even longer rails, but they have to be de-stressed. They will need to be lifted on to rollers and heated with gas burners until they stretch to the length they would be at a temperature midway between the lowest winter and highest summer levels. The assistant district engineer assures his inspector that all this has been done at other places and usually works quite well. He adds that the elimination of fishplate joints will provide a homogeneous track structure whereby every sleeper will need the same amount of maintenance, permitting it to be done by machines. The lengthmen wonder about the future of their jobs and the inspector comments that machines will have to be bloody good to do a better job than measured shovel packing.

Our train is reunited with its brake van and departs. An Aberdeen to Edinburgh passenger train passes by slowly behind a Class A2 steam engine, its crew aware that the coming of the diesels has heralded their own footplate revolution. I just feel lucky that I witnessed the start of something new.

Ferry Admiral

In his new post, Bryan Stone found himself responsible for the passenger service operated across the River Humber by three veteran paddle steamers.

In the 1960s the Doncaster district, where I had been a management trainee and now had some modest responsibility, was merged with the Lincoln district to become one of the new railway divisions. I was appointed as the passenger manager (commercial) so I quickly had to get to know Lincolnshire. In addition to some 100 stations, most on the Beeching closure lists, there was another quite intriguing mystery, listed in the Working Timetable as 'New Holland Pier to Hull (Steam Ferry)', worked by the Shipping and International Services people. As Hull was in another division it was certainly a frontier case.

At New Holland, on the south bank of the widening river, a ferry to Hull had existed for centuries. In 1836 the Lincoln stagecoaches had run there for the Hull connection. In 1845 a constituent of the Manchester, Sheffield & Lincolnshire Railway (MS&LR) had bought the ferry and built a railway to New Holland, and also to the adjacent Barton-on-Humber, with connections from Grimsby and the Doncaster direction. By chance, the Great Northern Railway opened from Boston to Grimsby in 1848, before its future main line was ready, so the first GNR trains ran between Louth and New Holland. At the latter, there was a 1,375ft timber pier with

With the Humber Estuary beyond, two diesel multiple units stand at the platforms of New Holland Pier station. The parcels van is a reminder that the station handled local parcels traffic as well as its ferry passengers. (Bryan Stone)

New Holland Pier diesel shunter D2021 dealt with the coal supplies for the three ferry steamers. The small signalling frame, with its view of the estuary, controlled the points linking the platform lines with the central release line. (Bryan Stone)

two platforms and a ramp below for freight, later for cars and motorbikes. The Great Central Railway, succeeding the MS&LR, always maintained that this was its main line to Hull, and there were through trains to reach the ferry. The ferries, however, ran primarily for local travellers, seamen, shipwrights and others, crossing between Grimsby, Immingham and Hull.

I decided to inspect the Humber Ferry without delay. There were three 209ft, 556-ton paddle steamers in the fleet: *Wingfield Castle* and *Tattershall Castle*, built in 1934, and *Lincoln Castle*, launched in 1940 and put into service in 1941. While two vessels were at work, the third acted as spare or was employed on excursions. All were true steamers with coal-fired engines and awkwardly positioned firebox doors that required a lot of dexterity on the part of the stokers.

Welcomed on board by the captain for the twenty-minute, 3-mile trip to Hull, there was time for a coffee and to meet the steward, stokers and engineer. The passengers, up to 1,200 of them, were mostly on deck in good weather, or in the smoky and gloomy saloons, though the buffet was popular. There were around sixteen return trips per day. The Humber is heavily tidal with shifting sandbanks and at that period had considerable shipping traffic. These shallow-draught, highly manoeuvrable paddle steamers were ideal, but fog and wind could cause disruption. The Eastern Region public timetable wisely warned: 'Should any delay for low tides or other causes occur, passengers must proceed by the next available train.' Most regular users parked their car or bike at New Holland, and there was a regular Lincolnshire Road Car bus service to and from the ferry.

Displaying her traditional lines, PS Tattershall Castle *lies off New Holland Pier waiting for her next turn of duty. (Bryan Stone)*

It was another world, and I was, it seemed, in charge of the non-nautical aspects. It ran itself really, but revenue, fares and ticketing, along with complaints (mostly missed connections, overloading, or soot nuisance from the coal-burning boilers) sometimes gleefully sent on from Hull, were my worry; as was the storm of protest resulting from changed train times. We never lost anybody, although packing a load of sixteen cars on the afterdeck was not always scratch-free, but they were carried at the owners' own risk. I recall that the fare was about four shillings for a single, more in the saloon, but most regulars had season tickets.

When it became known at Doncaster that I had a serious obligation to inspect the working of the ferry, I was surprised at how often people would look in with a good reason for coming along. It was a popular outing. I also learned that behind the scenes I earned the epithet of Admiral. For me it ended in 1968 when I left Doncaster, but the paddle ferries soldiered on until 1969 and the 1970s, delays to the Humber Bridge meaning that a vessel from Lymington had to be employed until 1981.

Despite being the youngest of the three, *Lincoln Castle* has failed to survive into preservation. All three had a period of chequered fortune after withdrawal from service, but *Tattershall Castle* eventually began a new life as a restaurant moored on the Thames, while *Wingfield Castle* was refurbished to take an honoured place as part of the Hartlepool Maritime Experience.

Show Time

From the time of Thomas Cook and the 1851 Great Exhibition, railways have served entertainment and events venues, and no event was more complex than the Royal Show, as Bill Parker reveals.

Summoned to the office of Cambridge district traffic manager Alan Suddaby, I was asked what I knew about the transport of animals by rail. Knowing he normally had quite a good sense of humour, I flippantly admitted to him: 'Very little; just shunting a few horseboxes, handling trainloads of Irish cattle coming to the Norfolk marshes for fattening, releasing pigeons on Mexborough station, and transporting human corpses in passenger and freight vans.' My first mistake, a rebuke and a lesson learned! I quickly realised what this questioning was leading to, namely the Royal Agricultural Show which in those days did not have a permanent site and was being held at Trumpington, near Cambridge. Much to my astonishment, I found myself in overall control of all the railway arrangements. I was also to be Alan's personal representative with the Show Committee and others of the agricultural hierarchy.

I found a little relief from the initial shock in learning that Geoff Herbert, who had just completed his traffic apprentice training, was to be my assistant. I knew he had a seemingly laid-back manner but was sharp and personable with an extremely dry sense of humour. My relief diminished when we met and I realised that he knew less about the railway role in this sort of grandiose event than I did. Nevertheless, I was subsequently most impressed by how Geoff coped with the Cambridge goods agent, who rather resented our involvement, and won him over by cleverly making our proposals look like they were his. Even more impressively, Geoff actively helped to save the day when a small group of animals, having just been offloaded, ran amok in the goods yard.

We learnt very quickly; our starting point being a series of briefings from district commercial officer Ralph Graveson on the intricate freight, passenger and parcels business requirements and our use of his sales staff. Then there was a short, sharp lesson about financial control and costs by district costing officer Bob Barron. Finally, on to the inimitable 'Mr Cambridge' himself, operator supreme George Docking, who in his forthright and definitive manner gave us an extremely helpful 'lecture', part of which was about our vital use of the district traffic inspectors Percy Baynes and Jimmy Greaves. To help matters, district motive power superintendent Geoff Parslew allocated a mechanical foreman and fitter to ensure the shunting engines kept running.

One of our first tasks, after an initial meeting with the local members of the Show Committee, was to manage for them the purchase of several hundred railway sleepers for transport to the then virgin showground field for making the internal roadways. We achieved this efficiently and helped to bolster our credibility with the experienced committee.

Our pre-planning liaison worked out well, with advance information about the contents of every wagon and despatch times by booked services or special freight trains getting through in a timely and systematical fashion. The task was not, of course, confined to the freight business. Arrangements had to be made for a large increase in passengers on booked and special services – all extra work, but not unusual for the Cambridge district office staff, who were accustomed to the extensive summer weekend passenger train workings. And the station staff, following the example of a most capable and enthusiastic stationmaster, revelled in the additional activity; so, too, did the British Transport Police in managing crowd control and the occasional drunkard.

There was great enthusiasm generally and in the depot goods office this brought out the wags who half-covered one of the walls with cartoons and captions. Some were very good, some were risqué. The only one I can recall was an imaginary scene with hordes of 'creatures' descending on Cambridge and a legend that included the phrase: 'and Noah descended on our fair city with his flocks in chariots but, praise the Lord, left his ark behind!'

From the incoming information we were able to determine staffing requirements. The Cambridge staff had the opportunity to work overtime and other volunteers were imported from our own stations and adjacent districts. We had to bring in extra road vehicles, cranes and all the ancillary equipment involved in the delivery of an incredible array of loads, from precious animals to gleaming machinery, all, understandably, more important to their exhibitors than anything else in the show.

The agricultural machinery ranged from tractors to combine harvesters, and the animals included high-quality breeds of poultry, pigs and sheep, as well as large bulls, a bewildering variety of cows, wonderful shire and graceful show-jumping horses. You name it, we seemed to have it, and every type of wagon was used to bring the array to Cambridge. Some of the smaller animals and poultry, together with materials for the exhibitors, came in as parcels traffic but, thankfully, were delivered from the passenger station.

About three weeks before the opening date the information on expected arrivals was transferred to a special control office located in the goods yard, which was led by the chief clerk and provided with staff on a twelve-hour shift basis. It was open twenty-four hours a day and before long accommodated goods depot and yard supervisors, also on a shift basis. From the information received of booked traffic and the planned train services to be used, this group pre-planned the depot handling, cartage and shunting and wagon placements. This, in turn, was completely co-ordinated with the show organisers. We checked we all had the same information, including the train and traffic arrival data. Based on this the organisers indicated when they would like the traffic at the showground, depending on the expected arrival times into the depot, the ability and time taken by the handling staff to empty the wagons and the cartage activity. These notional plans were reviewed and updated each night after that day's activities. It sounds complicated and there were hitches, but overall it worked out pretty well.

Our staff did a superb job, especially the inspectors, and the showground managers were equally able despite occasional impatient and aggressive demands from exhibitors. Such problems as did arise were dealt with, including some outside anyone's control. One example was a serious lorry/three-car collision on the main route to the showground which left the road completely blocked for a couple of hours. Another was a collision between private road vehicles and a crane in the showground, which resulted in the police blocking all incoming vehicles for about ninety minutes.

There was one incident that should have been simple to resolve but turned into a major event. A bolster wagon loaded with two gleaming, expensive tractors became derailed at very slow speed at hand points near the exit from the sidings. One bogie was completely off the rails, and one tractor was (as the man from the showground said in stronger language) leaning over precariously ready to topple over. It didn't seem so to me. Shunting and train movements had to stop due to the derailment.

Within minutes, the shed master and his mechanical foreman arrived, followed shortly afterwards by the district carriage and wagon foreman, the district civil engineer, the district operating superintendent Harry Crosthwaite and district motive power superintendent Geoff Parslew. Not unexpectedly, the news flashed around Cambridge and reached the media and the showground. A reporter and cameraman were allowed on to the site and the irate exhibitor arrived post-haste. And, of course, the steam crane (on standby) and breakdown van arrived.

There was quite an argument between the shed master and the exhibitor, who maintained that the tractors should be unloaded before re-railing or any wagon movement took place. It took around five minutes of heated debate before the shed master convinced the red-faced exhibitor of the simplicity of re-railing the bogie without doing this. Nonetheless, it was done cautiously, with all eyes on the precious tractors. Quickly back on the track, all was declared well and the wagon was moved into the goods depot at a snail's pace and surrounded by peering, anxious railway bosses and the tractor exhibitor. I found it much like a solemn funeral cortège, rather overdramatic and most amusing, and had to suppress a grin at the irrepressible Geoff Herbert's rather risqué description of it all.

All the meetings we had with the show's organisers proved them able, enthusiastic and always appreciative people. Our own staff displayed energy, professionalism and resourcefulness, and the exhibitors were a good bunch on the whole. Altogether, it was a most interesting experience and a great pleasure. A highlight, understandably, was being involved in the royal train arrangements and having the privilege of being in the line-up at the station to greet the Queen and Duke of Edinburgh when they visited the event.

distant sidings, auxiliary instruments to cater for distant locations, loss of a token etc. all had to be understood. If more trains passed one way than the other in a week, the signal and telegraph department lineman had to rebalance the two instruments involved by using a special 4-4-4-4 signal between them.

I have good memories of my visits to Clare, including a day when I worked the box myself. It was a pleasant, traditional station with two platforms serving the passing loop and then single lines east to Cavendish and west to Stoke. There was a level crossing one side and an intermediate siding on the other, plus a goods yard and two-line dock. The next day, my work at Haverhill signal box was rudely ended by the need to get back to Trumpington, where a morning coal train on the Up Goods line had taken the Up Passenger line signal as being its own, with the result that its J Class locomotive was derailed, overturned and buried under several coal wagons. The breakdown crane had to inch forward for the final lift as the track was repaired and each derailed wagon was lifted from the pile and placed in the adjoining field.

Further signal box visits and the able instructions of other district inspectors embraced acceptance lever working between Godmanchester and Huntingdon, and signal boxes in more complicated locations around Peterborough, Ely and King's Lynn. After all this training I had to test my understanding and competence by working a signal box in real time – under supervision, of course. The burden of watching me fell to the signalman at Kennett on the Bury–Newmarket line. It was a good choice and conventional in the sense that there were separate Up and Down lines and the standard pattern of three signals on each: Distant, Home and Starter.

The attractive passing loop station at Clare probably changed little over its century of working life. Its cosy signal box on the Up platform controlled the single line sections east towards Long Melford and west towards Haverhill and Cambridge.

I fell easily into the pattern of responding to 'call attention', 'is line clear for …?', 'line clear', 'train entering section' and 'train out of section', with the signals pulled off in order and replaced after the train tail lamp had been clearly seen. The times went into the train register, nothing untoward occurred and I went back to my Cambridge garret lodgings well pleased. By this time I had got the hang of 'pulling off', for without this knack a very distant signal involved a lot of wire and rodding and, however well counterweighted, was still a challenge.

Magdalen Road signal box was selected for my final test of competence. It lay on the main line just south of King's Lynn with the single-line branch to Wisbech leaving just beyond. Working it was really just an amalgam of previous experiences, although there were adjacent level crossing gates and station trailing crossovers to consider. Worryingly, there was also thick fog on the day I was there and I experienced a few moments of near-panic when the pick-up goods train started whistling from the fog-shrouded goods yard. I could see nothing. Did he want to be let out? Was the whistling for me or the yard staff? How many wagons had he got on, and would he 'run' if I let him proceed? Where was the Down Passenger train? And if I let the goods out, would it get clear of the passenger service and avoid both delay and the inevitable inquest?

Fortunately I caught sight of the Stop and Think collar on the signal lever controlling the exit from the goods yard and knew I must do just that. Information before action was the key and I must first contact the yard foreman or pick-up driver and then ring Stow Bardolph or Downham to find out where the passenger train was. As it turned out the goods was ready, but I was now offered the main-line train so it got the priority it should have. Lesson learned, and I still have a Stop and Think signal collar mounted and in clear view in my study.

A single-line tablet and token, and a signal lever collar used to give a warning reminder of possible conflicting train movements.

Unforgettable Meal

Most railwaymen will have had memorable meals on the move. Here, Basil Tellwright describes a meal conjured up in the most difficult of circumstances.

Back in the early 1960s, when I was working in the Liverpool Street Division, I had to go to a meeting in York during January. It finished about 17.00 and I walked the short stretch to the station knowing that there had been snow and sub-zero temperatures in the north-east for some time. I arrived to find that all trains were running late and even the Down trains were caked in ice. Luckily, I had only to wait a short time before a late-running Up train pulled in. It had snow on the roofs and the coaches were covered in ice. The steam heating was full on, an ice-free patch was visible low down on the body sides marking the location of the compartment heaters, but the windows were completely opaque.

The restaurant car stopped opposite me and, hoping for at least a hot drink, I boarded. I was greeted by a cheery steward who ushered me to a seat. The coach quickly filled up and the same steward came along and told us there was no printed menu but the kitchen could provide soup and a choice of steak and chips or grilled fish and chips. By this time we were on our way, heading into a snowy, icy night with a thin coat of ice forming on the inside of the windows.

Once all the orders had been taken we waited for a short time and then three stewards appeared like magicians: one was carrying soup plates wrapped in a hot towel; one had a steaming, bubbling soup tureen; and the third was placing the soup plates and filling them with soup. Rolls were delivered and the soup proved incredibly hot and delicious.

As soon as we had finished, the tables were cleared and the main course served in the same manner – wrapped plates, steaks that were sizzling hot, as were the fish and chips. There was no dessert but a running supply of coffee all the way to King's Cross. The contrast between the worst of winter conditions and the provision of a quality meal under such circumstances was a memorable experience that would be hard to equal.

Motorcycle Stationmaster

Stationmasters required to supervise a group of rural stations sometimes had their own transport problems, as Alex Bryce found out at Luthrie.

As a young relief stationmaster in the early 1950s, I was required to provide sickness relief for the stationmaster at Luthrie on the North of Fife line, including the stations at Lindores and Kilmany and freight sidings at Ayton and Rathillet. The staff at Luthrie included a bright but rather brash junior porter who early on pestered me about when I wanted to make use of the 650cc AJS motorcycle, which was provided for the stationmaster to visit outlying parts of his rural appointment.

The normal routine was for the visits to be made every Friday and accordingly the junior porter wheeled out this former Isle of Man TT model with the assumption that I was a competent motorcyclist and knew what was expected of me. Not so; my initial attempt to start up the engine produced no life at all and I secretly hoped there was a problem that would prevent me from using the machine that day. The helpful junior porter, however, pointed out I had not operated the petrol switch, and after he demonstrated what I had to do, the motorcycle was ready to take to the road.

As it was the first time I had ridden a motorcycle I set off very cautiously with my young instructor calling words of advice on how to control the machine and shouting directions to the outlying stations. All went well until my return to Luthrie station, when I perhaps rather too confidently speedily ascended the approach road on to the loading bank. Failing to brake properly I ran off the bank and crashed down on to the track below. I was fortunate to avoid any serious injury but the motorcycle was badly damaged and I hoped could not be replaced during the remainder of my time at Luthrie. But it was not to be; two days later the road motor engineer provided another motorcycle, probably encouraged by the junior porter who had emphasised how important it was for his stationmaster to have a replacement machine immediately.

Fortunately, the second motorcycle was much easier to operate and I became quite accomplished in using it, although I had an unhappy experience during an evening out in Dundee. I found on my rail return journey from Dundee to Wormit that the motorcycle would not start and I had to virtually push it over the 4-mile road route between Wormit and Kilmany station, where I was lodging with the family of the grade one porter. It was only a minor fault as I awoke later that Sunday morning to the sound of the motorcycle engine being revved up by my landlord and apparently in good order.

This period has been my one and only experience of motorcycles and I am happy to say I lived to tell the tale.

Now There's a Funny Thing

When Jim Gibbons was operating manager at Brighton a driver told him this story.

'Now there's a funny thing' was the catchphrase of the comedian Max Miller. He was a leading member of the Crazy Gang who, in their heyday in the 1950s, played regularly at London's Victoria Palace theatre, just across the road from Victoria station. Many of the performers lived on the Sussex coast, in or near Brighton, and after the show travelled home on the famous Brighton Belle Pullman, along with many other London theatre-goers.

One member of this band of regular travellers was reputed to be rather mean and this featured in the driver's story. The event he recounted took place one evening when he was working the late night Belle and waiting for the right-away from Victoria. He was approached in the cab by another member of the group who offered him a ten-shilling note to stop briefly at Preston Park, a station about a mile from Brighton and not served by fast trains, certainly not the Belle. It transpired the group members regularly took supper on the train and, to save the steward making out individual bills, took it in turns to pay for everyone. Apparently, the miserly member frequently managed to avoid taking his turn.

Despite the anonymous setting, this official photograph captures the unique special character of the Brighton Belle Pullman train.

The driver accepted the money, commenting to me that 'ten bob was a lot of money in those days', and stopped the train at Preston Park as requested. All of the conspirators got off, leaving their target as the only member left to settle the account.

Out of the Ordinary

Jim Gibbons vividly remembers some of the unusual happenings in Southern Region daily life.

Incidents Affecting the Working of Traffic – 24 Hours Ending 06.00

This was the heading of the daily Control Report compiled in each of the three Southern Region divisional control offices at the end of the night shift by the deputy chief controller. The DCC was, in fact, the shift manager and like a lot of railwaymen and women, particularly controllers, had his own idiosyncrasies. Some of them were not above adding their own humorous footnotes to odd items in the report and, provided they were not too numerous, a 'blind eye' was generally turned to these additions. One of my particular favourites read:

> 20.17 Victoria to Littlehampton/Portsmouth Harbour 25 minutes late start – British Transport Police called to train, passenger stated that he had been robbed in the buffet car. Not reported whether physical or Travellers Fare prices.

Hurried Exit

My chief operating inspector's brother was a driver and on the log one day he was reported to have climbed out of the cab window of his Class 33 locomotive due to the door being jammed shut. On reading this item my inspector commented dryly that this must have been one of the few occasions when his brother had climbed out of a window without his trousers over his arm!

We're Here to Help

Arriving at the office one morning I found a DCC in his best suit sitting in reception waiting to see 'the Guv'nor'. It transpired that on late turn the previous day, the Glyndebourne Opera House had invoked an arrangement whereby they contacted the DCC if an evening performance was running late and control made arrangements with Lewes station to hold the last Up London train. It appeared that the DCC had responded to the request for a twenty-minute hold with, 'I'll tell you what, lady. I'll hold the train for ten minutes and you get the band to play ten minutes faster.'

I gave him my opinion that he had not helped matters by referring to the Glyndebourne Opera Orchestra as a 'band'!

Ticket Barriers

Ticket barriers used to be manned by ticket collectors who were not above a bit of witty repartee, having already heard almost every comment ever made about the shortcomings of the railway industry. I was part of a team carrying out a passenger count at a London station one evening when a passenger rushed through the barrier saying to the collector as he passed through, 'Am I all right for Chatham?' To which the sotto voce response from our barrier representative was, 'Yes, sir. They're not too fussy down there.'

Before Mobile Phones

Divisional inspectors who had roving commissions were required to leave the details of their daily movements at a designated point. I was in a divisional Rules/Signalling & Accidents Section and we had geographically based area inspectors who were numbered, No. 1 area being the senior. Nos 1 and 2 areas were located in the same office block and so advised our section direct on the auto-dial telephone. The No. 1 area inspector was also a Justice of the Peace and, being the senior, left it to the No. 2 inspector to do the daily movement call, which often went something like this:

> I'm going to X,Y and Z signal boxes and the senior inspector's 'dispensing justice' on behalf of Her Majesty.

A 'Please Explain'

The Central Division of the Southern Region (SR) was in the process of introducing sliding-door Class 455 electric multiple units and driver-only operation. In addition to the obvious differences between the new units and our former SR slam-door stock, there was the parking brake, which was applied when the cab was shut down and released when the cab was energised by the driver. This obviated the not-unknown cases of handbrakes left on, particularly in intermediate cabs. On this particular occasion a driver terminated his train short of destination and took it into Selhurst depot without an explanation. The controller, in an attempt to establish the cause, suggested to the depot that perhaps a handbrake had not been released before departure. The depot obviously questioned the driver who faxed the following report direct to control:

> **Where is the handbrake on a 455?**
> To drive a train from London is not that hard
> Working DOO means we don't have a Guard
> So it's left to Control to get a slice of the action
> By saying the driver don't know his traction.
> They say he drove down from London with his handbrake on
> But on reaching Norwood, my handbrake had gone!

Is it at New Cross Gate, Brockley or Honor Oak Park?
I bet some lousy vandal's thrown it off for a lark
We carried on to the top of the bank
The Driver's skill is all you need thank
Our first stop at Norwood, we managed to make
But the mystery remains – where is that brake?

Who are these Controllers we never see
The things that they ask could crucify thee
Should we charge them with slander or libel maybe,
But knowing the system they'd be given redundancy.
Ask for a reason they duck and they dive
Please somebody tell them about the handbrake on a four-five-five!

Prison Yard

Bill Parker remembers when, as King's Cross divisional manager, he had the most unusual and fascinating task of helping to establish a prison.

It started with a telephone call from a well-respected professional colleague, Eastern Region estate surveyor Douglas Leslie, saying that the Home Office were looking for land on which to build a top-security prison. Before he could say any more about this request, both of us in perfect unison instantly said 'Whitemoor'. It was probably the quickest agreement of all time between the Property Board and any other department of BR.

By this time in the mid-1980s, the magnificence that once was Whitemoor marshalling yards, which I had known as general assistant to Cambridge district traffic manager Alan Suddaby in the late 1950s, had deteriorated into a massive wilderness eyesore. Of its 64 hectares, only a small area of a dozen or so marshalling sidings remained in the south-eastern corner. The infrastructure ironwork had been removed from the rest of this vast site, which had become overgrown with long wild grasses, weeds, shrubs and bushes. The soil was, I was told, so poisonously impregnated with various chemicals, oil, grease and coal that it had been unmarketable for housing, industrial or other building developments; neither was restoration feasible financially nor practicable to farming. Earlier attempts at a sale or lease had been unsuccessful.

We instantly and unanimously agreed with great enthusiasm that this opportunity for development must be given a top priority and 'all the stops pulled out' to achieve success. The allocation of responsibility was quickly decided: obviously Douglas and

Whitemoor Junction signal box, with its 117-lever frame, stood between the former marshalling yard and March station. It controlled the many train movements to and from the south end of the yard and the GN&GE Joint Line and on the Wisbech branch. (March and District Museum Society)

his Property Board colleagues would be in the lead in the negotiations with the Home Office; I took on the liaison role with the local authorities, the media and the community in what could be a highly sensitive project – there was the potential for a Nimby reaction at having a top-security prison on the immediate outskirts of the town and housing areas.

About a month afterwards a site visit was arranged for Home Office officials, to be accompanied by myself, Douglas Leslie and the divisional civil engineer, Mick Phelps. Recognising that a prison at the northern end of this massive bulbous-shaped wasteland, i.e. at the end furthest from the town, was an unlikely runner, we decided to try to influence the Home Office officials to select a site as far from the town and housing as acceptably practicable without prejudicing the development.

On the great day we, along with the three Home Office representatives, parked our cars out of the way on the western side of the area, just off the Guyhurne Road. We were dressed at Mick's instruction in protective clothing and wellies, and wore steel helmets. Not a pretty sight as we trudged through wet undergrowth to a suitable vantage point, the ruins of a former shunting control tower – that of the Down Yard Hump. This clear-visibility day with a strong cold wind prompted me to say jocularly that this location in fenland could be very bleak and could possibly be a deterrent to prisoners escaping. I was mildly rebuked by a straight-faced official who said 'Her Majesty's guests do not escape from high-security prisons'!

It was evident that the officials were keen on this area, with the prison some distance from the town, houses and railway station, the small traction depot and the group of residual freight shunting sidings. Access would also be well clear of the town by virtue of a new eastern access road. We parted from the meeting confident that this project would happen. The prospect of a prison had obviously been kept highly confidential up to this point. Negotiations by Douglas with the Home Office officials brought forward a reasonably clear indication that the prison really was 'on the cards'. So when would the planning authority, Fenland District Council, with its councillors, officers and others, including railway staff, be brought into the picture?

I was anxious to get the now likely project known to the local authority and community at the earliest stage. The solution to my dilemma over choosing the right moment was subsequently taken out of my hands. There had been no leaks but the site inspection party had been spotted by several staff from the shunting sidings and locomotive refuelling point. They had an inevitable and understandable curiosity about the reasons why these strangers were wandering through that wilderness. Something must be afoot!

The observation must have been passed around the railway staff and it reached the ears of one railway driver who was also a well-respected district councillor. We had developed a good working relationship and he had the confidence to telephone me about the strange visit and the ensuing rumours. Such was my trust in him that I readily gave him a brief résumé of the situation. Another positive development came from Douglas Leslie, who reported that the negotiations were progressing extremely well.

My train driver/councillor contact and I agreed it would be pertinent to instigate a meeting between the leader and senior councillors, officers, town dignitaries, Douglas Leslie and myself. March had been a strong, dynamic railway town, and despite the closure of the vast marshalling yards and the consequent job losses in all departments, it still had many former and current railway people and their families living in the town; the railway ethos had not gone.

I was surprised and delighted at how constructive and supportive the meeting was. Obviously there was the inevitable serious concern about having a top-security prison close to the town, but our arguments were debated openly and at great length, and in a most amicable manner. We stressed the benefits to the town, local businesses, employment and local economy, and the fact that without this development the land would continue to be derelict and become even more unsightly. Further progress meetings followed, some with Home Office officials present to emphasise the security and safety aspects, thus strengthening the case for the development.

Our reasoning pro-prison was accepted, appreciating that the community at large would need convincing of the merits of the project. We jointly agreed a plan, with each party having specific roles and liaising continuously to ensure accuracy and honest communication methodology. My public relations officer David Burridge played a strong role and gained great respect in the process.

I was delighted when planning approval was given to the prison. Together with the later developments of a business park and a large Network Rail engineering depot, the old and well-respected marshalling yard site I had once known moved from being a wasteland to a place of value again.

Merthyr Tydfil

Hugh Gould had vowed never to work in Cardiff but then spent two of the happiest years of his career there, beginning with a couple of incidents at Merthyr.

In 1985, only a year after the abolition of the divisional offices and the relocation of Western Region HQ from Paddington to Swindon, it was decided to abolish the regional passenger manager posts and redistribute their work among the new sectors, which were the 'flavour of the era' at that time. I was redundant for exactly one day before my new general manager, Sidney Newey, asked me if I would like to go to Cardiff as manager (Wales) with a remit involving the rather sizeable liaison job with the political world there. I had always vowed never to work in Cardiff, without knowing why, for I had travelled from Pontypool Road to Neath and had a passable knowledge of the valleys geographically. Anyway, I changed my tune with alacrity and found within days the remarkable affinity between Cardiff and my home city of Glasgow – something to do with 'attitude London', perhaps! And the last two years of my career were very happy indeed.

One of my tasks on arrival at Cardiff was to launch the GW150 Exhibition Train on a visit to Merthyr Tydfil in the July of the Great Western Railway's 150th anniversary year. This was part of a tour lasting from 19 May to 20 September 1985, during which the train and its coaches, fitted out with displays covering the whole history of the GWR, was open for public inspection at the main towns in the Western Region area. On reaching Merthyr I was appalled to find panic in full swing. The night before, when the train had arrived, it had been shunted rather too vigorously into the platform and most of the carefully arranged exhibits had collapsed. A bad night had been had by all, working frantically to reassemble everything in its rightful place, and order was only just being restored when I arrived. It was a close-run thing as right on my heels was the largest collection of mayoral chains of office I have ever seen. They have a lot of mayors in the valleys! We survived, but perhaps the close shave unnerved me for the sequel.

During the Exhibition Train visit I was presented with a copy of *Children of Cyfarthfa: Iron Horse* by its author; the book is set in Merthyr Tydfil in Trevithick's time when Cyfarthfa Iron Works were the heart of the heavy industry in the area. I was amazed to read that Merthyr then had a population of 40,000, whereas Cardiff had only 4,000. Needless to say, this has affected my view of Merthyr Tydfil ever since and when BR was invited to sponsor a day at the Junior Eisteddfod to be held there I readily agreed.

Then came the catch. 'Please do not be an absentee sponsor. Will you attend at least some of the proceedings?' I was asked.

'Yes, certainly,' I responded.

'And will you say a few words?'

'Of course. Happily,' I had agreed, before it dawned on my slow brain that the few words would have to be in Welsh. And no words are too few in Welsh!

I went to my friends at the Wales Tourist Board who shared Brunel House with us in Cardiff, some of whom I knew personally from my days in Europe working jointly with the British Tourist Authority. It was agreed that I would write down what I wanted to say and they would translate it into Welsh. The plan seemed fine. I worked hard to memorise my party piece, but on the day my courage failed me and I read from the lectern. Even so, I like to think that BR left a tiny mark on some young souls that day.

Peter Pan

The unimaginative would scoff at the idea of a locomotive having a dubious personality; not so David Maidment.

In November 1982, much to my surprise, I found I'd been appointed as chief operating manager of the London Midland Region (LMR), based at that hallowed place, Crewe. I'd gone my whole career – twenty-two years at that time – without setting foot on the LMR in a working capacity, and eleven years outside the operations function, so to say I was surprised is perhaps an understatement. And a Western man at Crewe? That was considered sacrilege by many, although I did hint that they had not done so badly with Sir William Stanier. After swatting up on track circuit block signalling and discovering where my rulebook was kept, I ventured forth on day one to the general manager's Monday conference, or the GM's 'prayers' as it was known.

The region's management was dispersed – operations at Crewe, mechanical engineering at Derby and general management at Euston – so the GM's regular meetings were compulsory for all of his team. I travelled up from Crewe to Euston House in the morning trying to make sense of the wodge of papers thrust into my hand as I left the office; not only the agenda and various items to read, but the closely typed twenty pages of train punctuality performance of the previous week. It had been left to me to analyse and make sense of it on the train journey, before I got shot down in flames by the engineers who, I was told, would gang up and blame the operator for everything if they could get away with it.

After this first meeting I returned to Crewe on the 18.05 Euston–Preston/ Blackpool and, feeling the need to take an interest in my new empire, noted 1965-built a/c electric locomotive No. 86259 *Peter Pan* at the front end. It had been named to celebrate the UN Year of the Child a couple of years previously. We got only as far as Wembley before we came to a halt and an ominous silence reigned. Eventually, after a delay of seventy minutes – when we were only a mile from Willesden traction depot – No. 87028 *Lord President* appeared, which was coupled on ahead of the failed locomotive and we continued north. Leaving Rugby, we suddenly ground to a halt again and it turned out that 87028 had now expired, and worse, had experienced brake problems that proved it impossible to release.

Time ticked by and I was furiously trying to think of what to do to avoid total disgrace on my first day in office. We were finally dragged back into Rugby by a Class 86/3 – another less-than-popular variant of this class of electrics due to its rough riding – leaving the two disabled electrics on the Down Main just beyond the Birmingham line flyover. Enthusiastic in my new duties, I then offered help to the guard and went through the front half of the train explaining what had happened and offering to take messages – it was before the days of mobile phones. The new locomotive eventually got us to Crewe just before midnight, four hours late. By the time I alighted I had fifty-eight messages to pass on from the Crewe booking office telephone. The front coach was full of French children on exchange visits to families all over Cumbria, and two gentlemen implored me to advise their wives of the reason for their delay as they would not otherwise be believed! It was nearly two o'clock in the morning before I remembered that I'd forgotten to ring my own wife, and it was with some trepidation that I opened the door to my home, but found she was fast asleep without an apparent care in the world.

Electric locomotive No. 86259 Peter Pan *at the head of a rail tour bound for Preston, where steam locomotive No. 48115 would take over to Carlisle. By this time, 86259 had been renamed* Les Ross *after its Birmingham DJ owner, and it performed well! (David Maidment)*

The next Monday evening I caught the 18.05 again and No. 86259 was once more the locomotive, and it failed en route yet again. Crewe Control realised that this loco was my bête noire and started warning me, and my wife, when it was in danger of appearing on a train I was due to take. When, a couple of years later, the Great Eastern Anglia section demanded four of our electric locos for crew training from Liverpool Street to Norwich, Crewe Control with some irony selected Nos 86259 and 86416 *Wigan Pier*, and I gather one of them pulled the wires down in Liverpool Street station on its first visit.

I subsequently had a number of perfectly adequate runs behind No. 86259, including cab rides, as I made it my principle to ride with drivers as much as possible; they used to complain that they only saw management when they were 'on the carpet'.

Now, in 2012, I see the occasional Class 86 during my regular Pendolino trips to London on Railway Children or Amnesty business, usually at Pete Waterman's Crewe LNWR depot. There are a few 86/6s used by the Freightliner business and a couple of preserved engines – No. 86101 *Sir William Stanier* and No. 86401 *Northampton Town*. But which is the one that regularly graces the charter trains from Birmingham or Euston to Crewe, before the steam loco takes over? Why, it's *Peter Pan*, of course! It has since metamorphosed into *Les Ross* after the Birmingham DJ who now owns it, via a ridiculous interim name glorifying some celebration in Manchester, and I had the pleasure recently of supplying Les with the details of its nefarious past. But to me it's still *Peter Pan* and I have the sort of rough affection for it that one feels for a naughty but precocious child. But I can't help wondering, when I'm tempted to embark on one of Tyseley's rail tours with Bob Meanley's splendid Castle or Princess steam locomotives, whether I shan't be marooned by *Peter Pan* yet again.

Sitting on the Fence

Being asked to report on services which two senior managers disagreed on was always going to be a no-win situation for a young man in training, as Alex Bryce found out.

As a Scottish Region traffic apprentice in the early 1950s training alongside Bert Gemmell, later chief passenger manager of the Eastern Region, York, we became involved in a disagreement between the general manager of the region, James Ness, and the chief operating manager, Freddie Margetts. The chief operating manager (COM) had introduced major changes in the Glasgow to Aberdeen InterCity services to achieve significant reductions in the journey times between the two main cities. This was brought about by a radical cutback in the number of stopping points, which required sensitive public relations handling with the local authorities and regular travellers as it also affected passengers heading to other principal stations on the route. The initial few weeks of the new timetable revealed it was badly flawed, with chronic unpunctuality giving rise to a barrage of complaints from travellers.

The COM decided the timetable changes were too ambitious and planned to put back more running time into the timetable and sharply improve the timekeeping of the services by lengthening the overall journey times. This was not acceptable, however, to the general manager who objected strongly to this convenient operating solution and insisted that the original planned improvements must be maintained by tighter and more disciplined punctuality.

Bert Gemmell and I were instructed to attend a Monday morning meeting with the general manager, James Ness, in person about the differences that had now arisen. We were detailed to carry out an in-depth study of the operation of the new timetable. He indicated quite clearly that he would anticipate our coming down in favour of the new timetable being maintained but with improved supervision to eliminate the delays.

Later that same morning Bert and I were summoned to visit the COM, Freddie Margetts – a formidable and very competent figure, who gave us a comprehensive briefing on why the timetable plan was not working and how important it was that the additional running time should be put back into the schedules. We were left in no doubt as to what he expected from our report and it was equally clear that this was not what the general manager wanted. We were in trouble!

At the end of the very limited four weeks we were given to report back, Bert and I agonised on how we could possibly come up with a solution that might be acceptable to both senior managers. Eventually, we came up with a masterly (we hoped!) compromise providing a measure of support for each of their arguments. The joint report we submitted was not something that we could be proud of and, almost inevitably, in our debriefing meeting with the GM and the COM we were criticised by each as having sat firmly on the fence.

Some good came out of the situation, however, as we were sent on an eight-week special exercise, which we had recommended in our report, as incognito passengers travelling on all the key Glasgow–Aberdeen services. We had to report in detail on all aspects of timekeeping and customer service standards by adopting the anonymous role of the most fastidious passenger – rather similar to the East Coast service inspectors travelling between Edinburgh and King's Cross – and embracing restaurant car services, station amenities and travel information facilities. We both hoped that this meant an escape from any adverse long-term repercussions as a result of our previous dilemma.

Whoops!

Tom Greaves little thought that a light-hearted suggestion would nearly become a reality.

One of the most important developments which enhanced the East Coast Main Line was its electrification, driven to a large extent by Don Heath, the project manager whose efforts earned him a well-deserved gong. Don is a delightful chap who has been a close friend and colleague for many years. At the onset of the electrification, partly to mock his single-minded drive, I light-heartedly commented that he should have the sense to electrify the Scarborough branch as well, something he chose to ignore. My view was somewhat biased as my home station was Malton, halfway down the line.

Shortly after my first retirement within the railway industry, slightly incapacitated by a broken leg and crutches, I was on what is now platform 5 at York where my temporary condition had been the subject of a little ribbing by two of my former carriage and wagon managers. The subject changed when locomotive No. 91001 appeared at the head of an InterCity line of sparkling white coaches; my comment to the two engineers was something along the lines of, 'what is that monument to insanity doing here?' Don Heath and I were committed supporters of the development of the Class 89 machines rather than the Class 91s.

Electric locomotive No. 91001 stands halted in the Scarborough platform at York after its trespass onto non-electrified track and a pantograph recovery task. (Tom Greaves)

The response to my rhetorical question was, 'It's on the first special train for the Institute of Civil Engineers and when it unloads we are going to give it the once over.' We then saw the locomotive move off with the intention of running round, but the road was set down the branch. All three of us uttered an appropriate expletive as the Class 91 de-wired and continued forward along the non-electrified beginning of the branch, its extended pantograph neatly trimming the wooden fretwork of the canopy over the curving end of the platform. This dramatic incident demanded camera action so the crutches were activated into full forward gear and I arrived in time to capture the displaced pantograph being hauled up from the ballast on to the station platform.

I left the scene and used the railway telephone to contact Don who fortunately was at his desk in London. I told him that the Class 91 had arrived at York. He knew about the special and asked if all was well. 'Sure,' I said, 'but you recall that I told you it would be common sense to wire the Scarborough line?' There was a non-committal cough before I added, 'Well, it has just taken that route as a light engine.'

Real concern was now apparent in Don's question about whether the locomotive was OK to work back; my reply was, 'Sure, providing that you put the pantograph back in the attic.' He took a further five seconds of convincing and then said, 'Right, leave it with me.'

Now, all railwaymen comply with the internal discipline whereby information is disseminated within the parish before being reported to a higher authority. Don's call to the chief operating manager of the Eastern Region, informing him of the disaster on his doorstep before his own control across the road did so, resulted in a conversation of a somewhat delicate nature.

The event did not quite end there as Captain Deltic of *Modern Railways* telephoned me the day after, referring to the photograph I had taken and asking for a copy for the next issue of the magazine. I thought it wise not to request credit and did not get paid either. Poetic justice perhaps!

The Swishing Fishes

Graham Paterson offers a 'whatever happened to' mystery – that of the Waterloo International Eurostar fishes.

When the public Eurostar service began in November 1994, there were ten gigantic mechanical fishes suspended from the ceiling of the Waterloo departure lounge. Initially, there were only a few services each day and, as the departure time for each approached, the fishes' tails began to swing ever more vigorously to alert passengers to head for the escalators up to the platforms. With the demise of Waterloo

International the fish ceased to swim, or swish. But how did they come to take up their illustrious position in the first place?

I understand that in October 1992, as Nicholas Grimshaw's award-winning international station was nearing completion, a public tender was launched by the UK's Public Art Commissions Agency. From the eighty architects' submissions the judges unanimously selected 'Channel Fishes', conceived by a celebrated French architect, M. Jean-Luc Vilmouth. Monsieur Vilmouth was well known for his interesting and innovative creations which were designed to 'reintegrate man and nature'. The fishes combined a certain gentleness with ecology, which in turn may have influenced Eurostar's later pioneering 'tread lightly' policies and actions. And, of course, the fishes' swishing tempo mirrored perfectly the certain sense of drama that accompanied each Eurostar departure.

Whatever happened to those fishes? Perhaps they never heard about the move to St Pancras International! Maybe they are still at Waterloo, waiting forlornly to join in the drama of the next Eurostar departure by swishing away once more.

Queen of Scots China

In the year before beginning his permanent railway career, Hugh Gould had an interesting time as a summer passenger guard at Glasgow Queen Street.

In my final year as a student in 1956, before joining the railway permanently as a traffic apprentice, I spent the summer as a passenger guard at Glasgow Queen Street. At that stage it had been the height of my ambition because I knew the additional Fort William duty in the summer timetable (which involved overtime) would be claimed by the senior guard in the depot, leaving a vacancy in the top link. This would not be filled because the other three links each had a night duty with enhanced payment, so nobody would move up. I had observed all this in 1955 when I was at Hyndland. Accordingly, I dropped hints in the right places at the right time and, as a result, spent the summer of 1956 in the Queen Street top guards' link.

It was a marvellous rota of six duties, rotating weekly: two on the West Highland Line (one Spean Bridge, one Bridge of Orchy); one to Thornton Junction (out via Dunfermline, back via Burntisland); one to Alloa; and two Edinburgh turns, the alternate duty finishing with the late duty 20.00 Waverley to Queen Street, which was the Queen of Scots Pullman.

One evening at Haymarket depot, instead of providing the usual No. 4 link 'any' locomotive (often a V2 Class 2-6-2) to take the Pullman to Glasgow, they turned out one of their prize A4 Pacifics, No. 12 *Commonwealth of Australia*, probably recuperating from a hot box problem. There was a snag, though. The Pullman set rarely saw A4s and the end couplings were therefore stiff. The leading buckeye coupling refused to engage until the third attempt, which was done with such force that the cupboard door in the Pullman kitchen flew open and its china contents smashed.

On departure, I was confronted by an unhappy Pullman conductor wanting my countersignature to his report, which was willingly given, subject to another minor snag. We had the same surname, which might have cast doubt on the authenticity of the rather unusual explanation he was being forced to give. At least Bob Gould was added to my lengthening list of friends.

When the Queen of Scots was withdrawn, Bob was transferred to the Golden Arrow; and ten years later, travelling to and from meetings in Paris, I used to see him aboard SS *Invicta*, on which he crossed daily to Calais and back in order to take reservations for the Up Pullman to London. He must have had quite a unique career, working to both Glasgow and Calais.

Also, in 1956, I had an interesting passenger guard duty involving the 15.09 Springburn to Balloch (Saturdays only), returning with the 18.40 Balloch to Bridgeton. Balloch Pier was, of course, the base of the beautiful paddle steamer *Maid of the Loch*, which had arrived to take up her Loch Lomond sailings some three years earlier. On my first trip on this train I was surprised to find that the return working had a different engine, one of the two V1 Class 2-6-2T engines from Balloch sub-shed. So, as prescribed, I went up to the front at the pier station to check the stops and train weight, and asked the driver his name. 'Conbrough,' he said, 'and I'll give you a bob if you can spell it.' As it happened, I had had a schoolmate called Conbrough, so I spelt it but magnanimously declined the proffered shilling.

Less amusing was my last trip on this duty when the superior (he thought) Eastfield driver failed to make a booked stop at Kilpatrick and I was too slow to notice. The inevitable retribution followed but at the normal pedestrian pace. When the letter foretelling my doom came before the staff clerk in Glasgow North district office, he, a former guard himself, was able to endorse it 'left service'. This was true, but he did not mention that I would be re-employed the following Monday on a permanent basis as a traffic apprentice!

Another choice moment of this period occurred when a celebrated Parkhead driver called Pickering, known to his colleagues as Two-Gun Bill and adept at torturing the English language, was awaiting departure at Balloch Pier one day. He remarked to his fireman, 'Doesn't the boat look awful big when they pull it up the slipway to scrape the tabernacles off?'

Biter Bit

Like everything else, management-staff relations were influenced by training skills and tactics. But two can play at that game, as Alex Bryce found out.

As assistant divisional manager at Wimbledon in the early 1970s, my duties occasionally involved me in local staff disputes, often arising from unofficial stoppages designed to disrupt evening peak services from Waterloo and cause major congestion at the terminal. It was important to prevent escalation of such disputes and early meetings with drivers' representatives were essential. The choice of meeting room and the agreed time of the more formal gatherings were critical; it was best to avoid early post-lunchtime and, if possible, restrict the negotiations to a small team from each side. We tried to deflect from open meetings where the staff supporters might influence the negotiators, some of whom tended to play to the gallery.

As a negotiating technique, the management side was often accused of having broken agreements or lied about previous discussions; this was designed to raise the temperature, disturb the management representatives and thereby influence the proceedings. There were one or two of the staff representatives who had a reputation for visiting the depots ostensibly to encourage conciliation, allegedly using 'petrol can' tactics.

At this time, many of those involved in industrial relations were sent on training courses to develop more skilled negotiating techniques. The Woking staff college, where many potential senior managers were trained, included Coverdale courses which had a strong psychological basis for leadership development in interpersonal relationships. For example, small groups of managers were set basic interactive exercises such as designing a floatable paper model or placing a pack of cards in maximum disarray. These simple exercises, monitored by a trained psychologist, revealed the personality traits of the various individuals, including those most assertive or least concerned in reaching an outcome to the exercise.

The use of certain gestures and mannerisms in industrial bargaining became a personal skill in negotiating meetings. It was argued that a close study of these habits of individual negotiators could reveal their personal reactions to propositions and perhaps provide a key to their strategy. For example, the tendency to lean forward or draw back in their seats, the clenching or unclenching of their hands, the significance of eye contact, all had a part to play in revealing what line they were following.

My personal relationship with some of the ASLEF and TSSA negotiators was on the whole very good and we generally showed respect for each other. But, after a particularly difficult negotiation with one of the TSSA team, when I had attempted to study my opponent's mannerisms, I was approached by the man in question as we left the meeting. He innocently enquired what I thought of the training courses that were now available for negotiating people. It transpired that he had recently been on a TUC course very similar to the one I had attended at Woking. He then confessed that he had assumed I was familiar with this training and had decided to set out to confuse me, adopting gestures and mannerisms contrary to what I might have expected. I think we both saw the humour in this situation, he more than I perhaps!

Coal Train Runaway

Philip Benham describes the dramatic saga at Corby when half a train of loaded coal wagons 'escaped' from Lloyds Sidings and set off along the main line.

Lloyds Sidings were situated adjacent to the blast furnaces and coke ovens of the steelworks at Corby. The site was curved and cramped, and the sidings were on a falling gradient to the north of 1 in 200. On 14 August 1975 a trainee shunter was sent to see the assistant area manager with a view to being passed out to take charge. As the Corby ASM this task would normally have fallen to me, but as I was on holiday, the relief manager, my great friend and mentor Maurice Ball, was covering the job. It did not take Maurice long to realise that the shunter was not ready, having an insufficient grasp of the necessary rules and regulations. He was sent back for further training, with advice on the areas requiring attention. Maurice told the yard supervisor that more training and a rules examination were needed before he was presented again with a Certificate of Competency for approval.

The yard supervisor concerned had a long and distinguished history on the working railway around Corby. He knew the yards and sidings like the back of his hand, and possessed an unsurpassed knowledge of the rail transport needs of the steelworks that dominated the town and was the reason for its extensive railway facilities. Railway work was not particularly well paid compared to jobs in the steelworks, and it was often a struggle to get staff to keep the job covered. When the shunter was sent back to the supervisor for further training and examination, his weaknesses were discussed with him. A few days later, faced with problems in covering the job, the supervisor decided the shunter was fit to take charge in Lloyds Sidings – a decision he did not mention to Maurice Ball.

Fast forward four weeks to the night of Wednesday 10 September. Train 8F10, the 21.10 Toton to Lloyds Sidings, consisting of sixty-eight loaded coal wagons for the coke ovens, had an uneventful journey until passing Manton Junction signal box. It was about 10 miles from destination and a red hand signal from the guard alerted the signalman to stop the train due to a hot axle box on one of the wagons. Following examination the train crew decided to continue at reduced speed to their destination, arriving on No. 1 Reception Line at Lloyds Sidings just after midnight on the Thursday. With trains of this length it was normal practice to divide them in order to assist in shunting the wagons into the main sidings. The somewhat inexperienced guard waited in his brake van as was usual, but, still worried about the hot box, set out after a while to report the matter. He did not think to apply the handbrake in his van before leaving it.

Meanwhile, the shunter of our story had set about dividing the train between the thirtieth and thirty-first wagons with a view to drawing the leading wagons forward into the shunt neck. As was commonplace in the days of short wheel-based wagons, all except the first few next to the engine lacked automatic brakes. Reliance was placed on the lever-operated handbrakes on the sides of the wagons, secured by pins placed into a vertical frame. The recognised practice for holding wagons detached from an engine was to pin down sufficient brake levers to prevent movement. Yet despite the gradient it did not occur to the shunter to pin down any brakes. To make matters worse, he had difficulty uncoupling and had to signal the driver to set back in order to ease the tension while he unhooked the couplings with his shunting pole. Released from the restraining engine, the rear thirty-eight loaded wagons and brake van set off down the gradient. Seeing what was happening, the shunter ran after them, belatedly attempting to apply some handbrakes. But it was too late and he had to give up, having only managed to secure one brake – nowhere near sufficient to stop several hundred tons of accelerating coal and metal!

As luck would have it, the following train on the Up line from Manton Junction – 8Z46, the 13.55 from Severn Tunnel Junction – was also headed for Lloyds Sidings. It had been held at Manton for some time while 8F10 had made its slow progress due to the hot box. As soon as 'train out of section' had been sent for the lame duck by Lloyds North signal box, the following train had been 'offered' and was now on its way. Signalman Telfer had quite correctly set the route from the Up running line on to No. 2 Reception Line, but in doing so, the normal 'trap' protection that would otherwise have prevented a runaway reaching the running line was removed. Even then, all might not have been lost had the signalman seen the runaway in time to reverse the points. Unfortunately, his view was obscured by another train approaching on the Down line and by then it was too late.

The time was 00.17 and the scene was now set for tragedy. Realising a collision between the runaway and the approaching 8Z46 was inevitable, Signalman Telfer sent the 'obstruction danger' signal to Manton Junction and rang Nottingham Control. Train 8Z46 was probably near Harringworth, about 4 miles away, when the errant wagons entered the running line. There was a signal box there but it was rarely open and was switched out at the time. Northamptonshire Police were alerted with the forlorn hope of warning the unsuspecting driver, but there was never a chance.

Immediately north of Lloyds, on the 5 miles of falling gradient to the Welland Viaduct, lay the mile-long Corby Tunnel. The accelerating runaway passed through the tunnel and collided with the engine of 8Z46 at the north end, at a closing speed later estimated at 60mph. In the dark, with a left-hand bend in the cutting approaching the tunnel, Driver Hartshorne may never even have seen the brake van tail lamps on the approaching mass of wagons; tragically, he was killed.

The mouth of Corby Tunnel on 11 September 1975, when runaway coal wagons came into violent collision with a train headed by Brush Type 2 diesel locomotive No. 31150. (Philip Benham Collection)

The diesel locomotive, No. 31150, was severely damaged with the driver's cab completely destroyed and the frame distorted. Damage to the errant wagons was also considerable, with no fewer than fifteen, all belonging to the British Steel Corporation, and the brake van from the runaway piled in a heap over the engine in the tunnel mouth. A further nine wagons from 8Z46 were derailed. All told, twenty-one wagons were damaged beyond repair.

The Toton 75-ton breakdown crane was alerted within minutes of the accident and was on site by 05.20, with a second 36-ton crane deployed by 08.20. The wrecked engine was drawn clear and the body of the poor driver finally recovered at 14.15; driver Sydney Hartshorne was a Leicester man, aged 57, and had completed thirty-eight years of exemplary service, having joined the railway in LMS days.

Re-railing was complete by 22.15 on the day of the accident. Clearing the site of several hundred tons of coal and checking the track took a little longer, but despite the fact that this was a freight-only route, the line reopened for traffic only four days after the accident. This was incredibly quick compared to modern times, when even top main lines can remain closed for weeks after any kind of serious mishap.

British Railway's internal inquiry, chaired by John Gradon, the divisional operating officer, was held at Nottingham the following week. The conclusion was not difficult to reach, namely that the vehicles had run away because they had not been properly secured. Responsibility lay jointly with the guard of 8F10 for failing to apply the brake van handbrake and the shunter for not applying sufficient handbrakes before uncoupling the wagons from the front portion of the train. Unforthcoming was any satisfactory explanation for the shunter being in charge when he was not fully competent. Although this was the result of the yard supervisor disobeying instructions, quite why was never really explained.

The accident had happened on my patch, and although I never faced any criticism, I felt a responsibility for what was clearly a failing in the management process. It was a salutary lesson for a young manager about the importance of staff competence, procedures and ensuring the paperwork was correct.

Subsequently, British Transport Police decided to prosecute the guard and shunter for endangering the lives of people on the railway. It took over a year for the case to reach Northampton Crown Court where, following presentation of the prosecution evidence, the judge ruled there was no case to answer.

On Call

Being 'on call' meant being available at any hour to deal with emergencies. Don Love describes two dramatic examples of on-call challenges he had to deal with.

One of the honours of working as a railway operator is being 'on call'. In my younger days I thought it was a privilege to be given the responsibility of part of the railway when higher management were tucked up in their beds. The essence of the system was that you could be called out by the control office or by one of your staff to any incident which disturbed the operation of the railway. My first job with on-call responsibility was in 1966 as assistant station manager of Streatham Hill, which covered part of the Brighton Main Line. This was before the advent of mobile phones and pagers so it was necessary to stay near a telephone and to live on or near the patch. The call-outs at station level were local problems: stations not opened on time by the early turn staff, derailments in freight yards or carriage sidings; rarely main-line incidents. The objective was to get things up and running promptly.

Divisional on call was another matter. When I became operating officer on the Central Division in 1970 I was called much more often, sometimes for a decision, sometimes to go out. The latter might involve a road journey to the site of anything up to 60 miles and then, once there, getting access to the line by negotiating fences, ditches and other obstacles. The trick was to get to the scene first before others arrived with their own priorities. My priority was simple: open the line for traffic by whatever safe means was available. I would describe the situation exactly to control and signalmen on the ground, tell them what needed to be done and how long it would take to clear.

In this lies a whole subject with which I tried to keep students awake at crew operating school, usually on the graveyard shift after lunch! Particular emphasis was on liaison with the engineers on site and on establishing causes. Each incident was different and therein lay its fascination.

I once arrived almost as the incident happened. I lived in Croydon and was called out at an early hour. An empty two-car electrical multiple unit had run away from Caterham platform minus crew and was running down the steep falling gradient on the branch towards Purley, 5 miles away, where there are sharp curves joining the Brighton Main Line. I dressed and telephoned control; the runaway had survived the curves at Purley, albeit at great speed, and was on the way to Croydon where the signalman would divert it into Norwood Yard to avoid the 1 in 100 gradient falling towards London Bridge, and hope for the best. The runaway lost some momentum but ran through the yard and out the other side, gracefully tangling itself up with the buffer stops at the end of the Up platform at Norwood, 9 miles from where it started and blocking the Up Loop. I arrived as the dust settled. Now to show my great expertise and clear the line before the morning peak! A shunting locomotive from the yard was hooked on and gave the errant EMU a bloody good pull. It wouldn't come. Cutting gear had to be called into play, and the morning peak came and went with some inevitable delays. Failure!

As was usual, I took the joint inquiry. The signalmen and control office had played it by the book, i.e. according to the 'vehicles running away on right line' procedures. The driver, as was the custom, had left the guard to apply the handbrake and place a shoe paddle over the wheel as a reminder that it was applied. The driver had then put the kettle on in the mess room at the buffer stop end and was joined there by the guard. They emerged a few seconds before departure time to find that their train had gone! The guard had not applied the handbrake and had never before done so at this location. He had failed to realise that the train was not the usual plain axle bearing stock which would not move on the almost level platform line; instead it was a new unit with roller bearings, a very different matter. It was his last day of service so the weight of the disciplinary procedure was not invoked, but I'm sure he didn't forget the incident.

I stayed on the Central until 1978 and one of the last call-outs I had in that job was at Victoria. It was Saturday morning and the coaches of an electric multiple unit boat train had split the points going into Grosvenor Sheds, coming to a stand over the rising gradient to Grosvenor Bridge and blocking the throat of Victoria (Eastern) station. Although this was in my division, it came under the tender care of South Eastern Control for train arrangements. My Central trains were happily going in and out on the other side of the station as if nothing had happened.

We needed the crane, which could only approach over Grosvenor Bridge and down the bank. The crane was duly ordered, some third rail hook switches opened, shoe fuses removed and handbrake applied on the derailed unit to allow the crane to operate and permit the restoration of current to some of the Eastern platforms. The rear of the train was on the track but buffer-locked to the derailed unit. So it was cut free and one buffer removed from the front unit. With the juice now on, the rear of the train was driven back to the platform. The rear unit now out of the way, a limited service could use the Eastern side.

The crane had arrived and started work. I was standing beside the front unit being re-railed when it started to move down the gradient towards the station. I ran after it – not easy over ballast and points – climbed into the cab and wound the handbrake some more turns. It bit sufficiently for the remaining buffer to just gently touch the rear unit in the platform. Phew! It was the result I wanted but not in that way.

While walking back towards the crane I saw a massive yellow flash and smoke where the permanent way men were straightening the track. The shoe fuses had only been removed from one side instead of both sides of the front unit, and it had juiced up the isolated section while running on to the live platform section where the third rail was on the opposite side. I did not feel too confident that my instructions were being understood.

I passed the permanent way gang who were recovering from flash blindness and as I walked up the gradient towards the crane, I was aware of guilty expressions on the faces of the re-railing men. There were pieces of splintered timber on the track. The crane had run away down the grade and the timber was the result of frantic, but successful, efforts to stop it. No one was injured; the flash blindness was treated by the medical officer and had no permanent effect. The job was done promptly, but after twelve years and countless call-outs, I wondered whether my luck had finally run out.

As usual, I took the inquiry; the primary cause was a worn switch. As for the other events, all I had to say was that 'the best was done'. My later jobs at Liverpool Street and British Railways HQ did not involve directly being on call because there were others to turn out. But that did not stop the telephone ringing! It is a cross the operator has to bear.

The Cloth

Deriving this informal title from their black garb and wide authority, all district inspectors accumulated a fund of railway stories, and Bill Parker was no exception.

My introduction to district inspectors (DIs) and their knowledge, responsibilities and authority was at an early age. During the visits of my uncle, the DI at Langwith Junction, Shirebrook, I was allowed to listen to him and my knowledgeable father – a relief stationmaster – discussing rules and regulations and railway operating practices. Subjects like 'six bells – obstruction danger' and 'train running away' were to me fascinating and exciting, far better than the *Beano* and *Hotspur* comics! Little did I know in those early days that when I grew up I would achieve the privileged and distinguished position of DI.

Reporting directly to the district operating superintendent (DOS) and his assistant, the DIs of old were unquestionably regarded as quite superior people, with exceptional powers over all operating department staff, and with senior operating officers depending very much on their competence, decisions and recommendations. During my time in two DI appointments, my basic responsibilities were supplemented by a few experiences very different from the normal routine.

One of my early jobs as a King's Cross district inspector was handed out by highly respected district trains assistant Bill Sterling. This was to improve the empty passenger rolling stock working from King's Cross station to Bounds Green coaching stock depot, in association with the depot master Brian Hamilton. And he wanted a full report within ten days. With the flamboyant and highly competent Brian, probably the best amateur comedy actor in Gilbert and Sullivan operettas in the country, we started with a route march along the tortuous approaches to the depot. We ended up with several low-cost suggestions which were accepted and resulted in speedier movements and staff cost economies.

Another job from Bill Sterling is memorable for an unusual reason. I was to investigate wagon utilisation and train operations at the Ashburton Grove (Highbury Vale) London County Council rubbish depot and at the destination site on the Welwyn Garden City–Hertford branch, to which the rubbish was conveyed in trainloads of wagons formerly used for brick traffic. This, I thought, would be quite a nice option, but naively I overlooked the nature of the business. On arriving at the depot I was horrified at the filthy scene and its foul stench. It was one of the quickest jobs I ever completed, and I was thankful I did not contract any nasty diseases.

On a cold, dark night north of King's Cross, during the making of the film *The Ladykillers*, I had the pleasure of being involved with chief district inspector Harry Beeby in organising the freight train working for the scene where the body is dropped into a freight train wagon.

One job I don't boast about was making a mess of some train working during a single-line working. A misjudgement on my part caused the pilotman to be at the wrong end of the section, causing delays to a couple of freight trains. Bill Sterling surprisingly let me off the hook and blamed his controllers for giving me incorrect information. But I knew differently – that it was primarily my fault!

The weekly DI meetings were held at Knebworth where the district operating superintendent's function was housed in a former wartime control building. Arriving there on one occasion, Reg Clay, the formidable staff clerk, escorted me to attend on Bill Green, the DOS. Bill kept me waiting before looking up and saying, 'I'm sending you home.' I was stunned, thinking I had been suspended, until he revealed that he was actually appointing me to the DI's post at Peterborough, where I had links. Reg Clay was stunned, too, by the absence of the usual formal interview and by being instructed to arrange my lodgings.

It was at Peterborough that I was involved with the royal train for the first time. Adorned in bowler hat and my best uniform, and in company with the shed master, I stationed myself at Spital Junction signal box where we received news that the train engine was faulty and had to be replaced. We hurried across the track in the semi-darkness to the country end of the Down platform to supervise the engine change process. Who should stroll into this area of high activity but the Duke of Edinburgh himself, asking, in his typical manner, about the faulty engine and how long we were going to be. My first ever audience with royalty was a bit daunting and would have been more so had I known that in my long railway career, an engine failure on the royal train would mark four of the many occasions when I was in charge!

While I was in the Peterborough DI post, my wife Barbara had a spell in Papworth Hospital and, although this was outside my geographical district, I was given carte blanche by the district operating superintendent to visit her whenever I wished. Despite the petrol rationing at the time, arrangements were made for a railway police car to stand by in case of a train working emergency. And, of course, there was an emergency and it occurred while I was visiting Papworth. The bank of the Up Goods line near Wood Walton, north of Huntingdon, had slipped, causing about 50yd of track to be suspended without any support, affecting the Up Main line. As the nearest district inspector to the mishap site, I was summoned into the matron's office and notified on Bill Green's instructions to go immediately to Wood Walton signal box and take charge until the Hitchin-based inspector, Ernie Amsden, arrived. This I did, but not by police car – by hospital ambulance with its siren blaring and lights flashing.

When Ernie Amsden arrived at Wood Walton, I had a telephone call from Bill Green. In his well-known, formidable, after-lunch manner the district operating superintendent's message was that 'he did not need two district inspectors to watch some so-and-so track waving about in the wind' and I was to go back to Peterborough. This, I remember, had been my intention, but Bill Green was not the sort of person to tell that to.

We had one serious derailment at Werrington Junction, north of Peterborough, where within my authority I 'adjusted' a number of rules to get the breakdown crane on site and expedite the re-railing. My unconventional action was endorsed by assistant district operating superintendent John Christopher, himself a former DI, albeit with the comment that 'had I been a clergyman I would have broken most of the ten commandments'! I also found myself added to the Christmas card list of the shed master and district engineer.

The district inspector fraternity did have a priestly air about it, with members dressed in black habits, but it was an important and respected group in the railway industry. Gerry Fiennes, probably the best operator I know, observed of DIs: 'They may look like crows and rooks in their bowlers, black suits and overcoats … but we cannot do without them … and it's a foolish senior operator who disregards them!'

Steam Pressures

Tom Greaves witnessed the increased pressure on the remaining steam maintenance facilities as the diesels appeared.

In the late 1950s traction depot life was far from peaceful. This was particularly so in the London area where steam maintenance and repair facilities were at a premium, particularly when away from the high-profile depots such as King's Cross and Old Oak. There, the express passenger locomotives had a far higher ratio of staff than that available for lowly freight with its aged locomotives, such as old GNR Class J52 'Starvers', J50 'U-boats', and the much-thrashed Austerities on the longer-distance workings.

Most steam locomotive types had 'informal' names deriving from their appearance or working. The J52 'Starvers' were a rebuild of a class which had its foundations in earlier Stirling designs and had a slightly larger boiler to enable them to challenge Ludgate Hill on the cross-London freight transfer workings. Their name originated because their increased loads meant fewer driving turns during a period of depression. The 'U-boats', the J50s, were another 0-6-0 class, also variously known as 'Ardsley Side Tanks' or 'Submarines', and took the name from

Class J52 locomotive No. 68961 exhibits a good head of steam at Hornsey locomotive depot. She was one of a 1926 rebuild of an earlier version. (Tom Greaves)

their long, sloped tanks. These tanks were connected by a balancing pipe which caused great problems during general repairs. The fitter could only tighten the outside nuts if a diminutive apprentice was dropped through the tank filler hole and then circumnavigated four water baffles to hold the bolt head to prevent it turning. I experienced this first hand and also the dubious prank of colleagues banging on the tank sides during the ordeal.

Hornsey was one of the depots under pressure from the introduction of a diesel fleet intended for the GN suburban workings, but despite all the problems the team there did very well. The pressure increased further when I was obliged to take two shed roads to accommodate the newly arriving diesels, which politics demanded should work 'straight out of the box'. The steam-bred management was understandably short of new traction experience and often less understanding of the shop floor pressures, which in some cases, King's Cross among them, led to a counterproductive steam versus diesel division.

My task of keeping things running despite these issues was eased with the help and understanding of Fred Hulme, the Hornsey steam depot shed master, who was a true gentleman. Fred ran his depot in a wonderfully laid-back manner built on years of previous experience at Woodford Halse. All was under control, helped particularly by his mechanical foreman Joe and relative isolation from the higher-level pressures which tended to be concentrated on the East Coast Main Line glory boys. This delightful north countryman was intent on maintaining his peaceful steam depot life.

The early months of diesel operation transformed the calm and stability of Hornsey depot and thrust it into the limelight. Fred expressed the change in an eloquent manner, addressing me with the comment, 'Mr Greaves, before you and your diesels came to Hornsey, every day was a Sunday, now every ****** day is a Monday.' Irrespective of this sentiment, he continued to assist whenever he could, the measure of a true railwayman.

We invariably had a coffee together in his office about eleven o'clock after the morning peak issues had been resolved. It was during one of these breaks that I learned a lesson in diplomacy from Fred. A major problem which he faced was that of steam locomotives raising a fire – 'brewing up' – to the considerable discontent of the householders in the adjoining streets and constant harassment from the council who were well equipped with the Ringleman charts of permissive smoke emissions. The J50s and 52s were very competent in making smoke! On one occasion a large North London housewife burst into Fred's office and draped a whole load of washing over his head, with the words, 'Now wash that bloody lot, mate.' Fred appeared unfazed by the onslaught. Still resting back in his easy chair and smoking his ever-present cigarette, with a pair of outsized knickers draped over his trilby, he just said, 'Sit down, lass, and we'll have a cup of tea.' He called for Joe to make a pot of tea, and added, 'Bring the chocolate biscuits in, as well.'

The lady in question left fifteen minutes later with her washing, quiet as a lamb; an example of depot life and a sound lesson in reactive diplomacy.

The Whirling Dervishes

A bizarre ritual, not at Khartoum, but still an eye-opener for Les Binns on the rather more normal Saltburn line.

I spent seven years as divisional operations officer in the very large Newcastle Division, which ran from Northallerton to the Scottish border and included Teesside and routes east of the Pennine Divide. It was large, also, in terms of its trade because it dealt with a major part of the East Coast Main Line and serviced heavy industries, including iron and steel at Consett and on Teesside, and two major coalfields in Durham and Northumberland. There were hump marshalling yards at Lamesley (Tyne Yard) and Thornaby (Tees Yard).

In this environment one learned quickly that good relationships between departments were essential if the work was to proceed smoothly. Departmental conflicts did exist, which was not surprising when you look at the opposing responsibilities of the civil engineer and the operators. The former required access to the running lines in order to maintain track and structures but at a cost of diversions, delays and speed restrictions, while the latter simply wanted to run a planned timetable all day and every day. Nevertheless, the many short-term arrangements for track work were sorted out by dialogue and concession, but I do remember one occasion that proved quite out of the ordinary.

It was when I received an unusual – almost rare – invitation to join the Newcastle divisional civil engineers in travelling on the inspection saloon over the Darlington–Saltburn line. Being asked was a first so I accepted with alacrity, while privately wondering what they were after. I joined my engineering colleagues at Newcastle Central and was surprised to see them dressed, quite frankly, like tramps. This was well before dressing down was in vogue and they all looked as though they were prepared for a garden bonfire. Oddly enough, each carried a briefcase and an ice axe, of the sort that climbers use.

We boarded an InterCity 125 train, newly introduced on to the ECML, and marched down the central gangway of a first-class saloon. The looks we got from our fellow passengers were as bizarre as our appearance. However, we behaved ourselves and everybody settled down for an uneventful journey to Darlington, where we joined the saloon. Meanwhile, I was privately musing on the engineers' objectives for the day; operators are good at musing; it helps explain the punctuality statistics!

The Darlington–Saltburn line was a segmented route with quite different structures and traffics. The first part from Darlington to Eaglescliffe was basically two-track, catering for a half-hourly diesel multiple unit service in each direction. Then from Eaglescliffe to Bowesfield Junction the line from Northallerton contributed a heavy south/north freight flow; at Bowesfield Junction the coast route joined up, bringing passenger and freight traffics from Stockton and Hartlepool. The route was quadrupled or more from Eaglescliffe to beyond the Redcar Ore Terminal, and this section included the two-hump Tees Marshalling Yard.

The saloon moved out along the two-track section between Darlington and Middlesbrough and we called at some underbridges and cattle creeps until we halted, roughly midway to Eaglescliffe, close to a pile of sleepers in the six-foot. Everyone piled out and I watched in total amazement as they all attacked the sleepers with their ice axes. It was a truly frenzied assault on the timbers and lasted about ten minutes. I did notice that we were on an embankment above a housing estate and wondered what the housewives would think if they looked out of their windows and saw the six Whirling Dervishes dancing round a pile of sleepers and wielding their weapons with such gusto.

Abruptly, the war dance ended and we re-boarded the saloon. After a few minutes I cautiously asked what all the activity had been about and I shall always remember the answer I got. It was, they explained, a numerate way of doing a rough check on the fitness of a section of track, giving an indication of when relaying might be needed. The local permanent way inspector would remove ten sleepers at random which would then be subjected to physical violence, as I had seen, to test their relative soundness. Scores would be recorded on a scale of one to five, where one was a very sound timber and five was a very rotten one. They then multiplied the score to give a number out of a hundred. From memory the final scale was something like, a score of over ninety meant the line had to be closed to traffic immediately, seventy to ninety required a temporary speed restriction, fifty to seventy justified some specific relaying within two months, while under fifty meant the line was fit until the next major renewal. I enquired, again cautiously, about the score they had arrived at that day. Just over fifty, I was told, along with a request for a possession. I had no choice but to agree. After all, when you are faced with six ice axe-wielding Whirling Dervishes, what can you do?

The Woking Ladies' Finishing School

The BR senior management courses at the British Transport Staff College at Woking involved eight weeks of intense application. Drawing from his memories of Course No. 16, Geoff Body describes a few of the lighter moments as well.

A junior management course at Windsor and the middle management course held at Derby were followed by my selection in 1966 for the next level: Course No. 16 at the British Transport Staff College at Woking. Once there, a civil reception and settling-in period was the prelude to eight weeks of near-unremitting study, instruction and scrutiny. Until the final evening, that is.

The imposing Woking venue for senior management courses at the British Transport Staff College (BTSC).

Twenty-two of the thirty-one people on the course came from the various departments and disciplines of the nationalised rail industry. The others were a disparate bunch, two from the Port of London Authority and London Transport, plus single representatives from the docks, buses and even the MoD. Two were from overseas: Louis Verberckt from Belgian National Railways (SNCB), whose smoking pipe was an integral part of his persona; and Bill Hinkel from Canadian National Railways, who quickly inveigled the unwary, myself included, into his barbershop quartet. The group got on well, each member contributing his own skills and talents.

The course list of obligatory reading was frightening but the overall programme was varied and excellent. There were some sobering moments, like the demolition and rebuilding of one member's stuttering speech by the expert in Effective Speaking. Brutal though the treatment was, it seemed to work. I found it somewhat distasteful, something better done in private, and on a later course a 6ft 6in former regimental sergeant major from London Transport expressed his disapproval in a similar situation by threatening to throw the lecturer down the stairs!

The only group outing, to Schiphol Airport and other transport locations in Holland, was useful and memorable. Memorable for the generous reception we received by fellow travellers for an impromptu song concert we performed while travelling on an Amsterdam tram; and for the pathetic sight of the group alighting from the boat at Parkeston Quay after three days of burning the candle at both ends and middle. Full of 'Geneva' rather than career promise!

Happily, our course was in the late spring with good light remaining after dinner in the evenings. As a change from our other safety valve – trying to outdo Secretary Claude Lincoln at Liar Dice – we could make use of the excellent croquet court.

By some element of luck I managed to reach the final of the course championship, only to find that my opponent was the principal. In the event, I lost narrowly, but I like to think it was nothing to do with currying favour for a good end-of-course assessment. I came to feel that croquet was a much-underrated game, which offered a wealth of opportunities to disadvantage opponents and had a propensity for quite vicious tactics.

The extent to which we had responded to the course input had to be determined and we were aware that we would be assessed to that end. And what better subject for the traditional end-of-course evening entertainment that we students had to put on? Hence we created the Woking Ladies' Finishing School, where our sketches threw caution to the wind and we staged a judging panel to assess the college principal and each of his staff. Bespectacled and seemingly earnest course members took up a thoughtful pose behind their table as each staff member was discussed, with notes taken by an accountant member who had been pressed into wearing drag for the part. There was no point in half measures so we were merciless. Even the urbane principal was labelled as 'showing some promise' but needed 'curbs on his wayward enthusiasms'. Only the catering staff escaped our scurrilous attention, for obvious reasons.

As part of our show, members had produced irreverent words for a dozen or so folk tunes, a few monologues and a selection of 'promotional aids'. My small

BTSC senior management course No. 16 has ended and those attending take up less serious roles in the customary end-of-course entertainment.

contribution was a poster depicting a tree with owls perched on each of its branches. The owl featured in the college crest and each of my 'owls' was a caricature of the individual course members. The owl for SNCB Louis was, of course, smoking a pipe. It was no great work of art but on a later visit to the college I was immensely pleased to find that in addition to being named on the boards recording each course and those who attended it, my poster had been framed to enliven the dining hall. The peak of any claim I ever had to artistic achievement!

One of the songs included in our concert comprised a set of fresh lyrics for *Men of Harlech*. In its revised form the words ran:

What's the use of Woking training,
Teaching things I'm sure are paining,
Academic thoughts engraining,
What a load of junk.
Management – a bookish theory?
Many a theme that makes me weary,
This belief is held sincerely,
It's a load of bunk.

Heed not this distraction; management is action!
Leadership, with firmer grip,
To counteract each trouble-making faction.
Managers will be degraded,
If these theories are paraded,
Of this truth I am persuaded,
Lowly have we sunk.

Sir, we fear you're misdirected,
Since this training you've rejected,
Now it's time you were corrected,
By the Woking School.
Very soon you'll be conceding,
If you do your proper reading,
All this training you've been needing,
Every useful tool.

Passing Information; Art of Delegation,
Business Ends and Market Trends,
Full Budgeting Control, Devaluation,
Consultation at your station,
Ring a bell at public peroration,
Even time for recreation,
In the swimming pool!

A Shade Too Far

Hugh Gould offered some advice to his signalman at Burntisland with some rather unexpected results.

In 1960, after a long wait for an appointment due to a shortage of vacancies, I suddenly became stationmaster of Burntisland including Kinghorn, working with some of the finest railway staff I have ever met. My two years there were very happy indeed.

The principal freight business at Burntisland was that of the British Aluminium Company, who imported bauxite ore through the docks. We then tripped it to the BAC works in mineral wagons, where it was transformed into alumina powder and forwarded to the West Highland factories, either in alumina vans of 1927 vintage to Fort William or modern Presflo wagons to Ballachulish, for onward transfer to Kinlochleven Works. The BAC complex was connected to the main line by a single-shifted signal box called Newbiggin. The signalman was a good-natured West Countryman called George who was totally reliable, but not the tidiest of souls. One day I arrived to find ash all over the floor, and decided it was time to draw the line. So I put it to George, gently and tactfully, that if he took a little more pride in his box, he might find he was happier at his work.

The effect was amazing. George went from one extreme to the other. Very soon the signal box was a model of perfection, until he went a step too far. One morning, coming up the stairs, I detected a smell of paint. Surely he could not have invaded the hallowed territory of the signal and telegraph department? But he had. Worse, the spare levers, a high proportion of the total frame, were now cream instead of white.

'George,' I said. 'What on earth have you done?' But George misunderstood my reaction.

'Yes, sir,' he said, beaming with pride. 'It's Dulux.'

I admit I enjoyed the 'sir'. I was young.

The North Briton

A great deal of attention was paid to the performance of this prestigious train, as David Ward demonstrates.

A recollection I have from the 1950s involves the way a total brake failure was overcome on the Leeds to Glasgow morning business train named the North Briton.

Neville Hill depot had an allocation of Class A3 Pacific locomotives for working this service and the Queen of Scots Pullman trains between Leeds and Newcastle, and great attention was paid to their reliability and punctuality. On this particular day the North Briton came to a stand at Sessay on the East Coast Main Line just south of Thirsk with total loss of brake vacuum. The fireman and guard started to walk down the train to listen for a leak.

David Lamb, the assistant district superintendent at York, was on the train. He got down to the ballast and insisted the correct procedure was carried out for finding the fault. This was to firstly disconnect the vacuum hoses between the engine tender and the first carriage, to put the tender hose on its stop and then ask the driver to create vacuum with the small ejector. If 20in of vacuum cannot be created on the locomotive gauge then the locomotive is the cause of the problem, which proved to be the case in this incident.

It is virtually level track on to Darlington, and the train formation had a brake van with handbrake at the extreme rear so if the district control at York and Darlington could ensure a clear line ahead, then the train could be worked at very low speed to Darlington, a distance of about 30 miles, without the continuous brake operating on the carriages. Control of the train would be from the guard's brake and the locomotive brake.

I cannot remember now whether sufficient vacuum could be created on the locomotive to enable its brakes to be worked by vacuum or whether the locomotive had to be worked unbraked, with stopping power from the front of the train having to rely on the tender handbrake and, as a last resort, the driver putting the locomotive into reverse gear and applying steam to the cylinders. Whichever was the case, the North Briton crept forward safely to Darlington, saved from major delay by an on-the-spot decision.

There was a small risk in working the train in this way, but the method was little different to the way the majority of freight trains were worked at that time. Today, such a method of solving a brake failure would never be agreed and substantial delay would occur to the train itself and to other trains until a replacement locomotive could be found and attached; in those days, however, it was an excellent example of a senior railway officer using his practical knowledge and taking personal responsibility for the decision.

Another interesting operational feature of the North Briton was the requirement for a carriage configured with half as open first-class seating and the other half as compartments, a vehicle referred to as a Semi FO. This was because the demand for full meals did not justify a full open carriage and in those days compartments were considered essential for non-meal-taking first-class ticket holders. Another reason was that on its southbound journey the North Briton was timed to run from Darlington start to York stop — 44 miles — in just forty-three minutes; at the time this was the fastest timing in the whole of the BR timetable. It was essential, therefore, to limit the load to nine carriages.

However, there were only three Semi FO carriages in the whole of the ex-LNER carriage fleet and another was required for the Master Cutler service between Sheffield and Marylebone, leaving only one for use as an emergency or maintenance replacement. In fact, control of the maintenance and overhaul of these three vehicles was, in practice, so tight and efficient that it was rare for either train to have to operate without its Semi FO. This was particularly creditable bearing in mind the set of carriages were diagrammed to run a round trip daily from Leeds to Glasgow of 555 miles.

Caught Out

The railway industry had its share of pranksters and Geoff Body was a victim on a couple of occasions.

My training schedule included a period at March motive power depot – not a glamorous place, but one of immense variety and interest which provided facilities for the workings to and from Whitemoor Yard, for the passenger services through March and for all sorts of branch lines and local duties. I was treated well and rather forgot the semi-obligation staff felt to test the mettle of traffic apprentices. In the running shed I built a locomotive brick arch under supervision and was then invited to try to find a fractured boiler stay by tapping the ends from inside the firebox. After half an hour of cramped tapping and listening, it finally dawned on me that this engine had perfectly healthy stays!

Much later on, and in a rather more elevated position, I attended a day of weighty lectures at Swindon. During one of these a large envelope was delivered to me with the message that it was highly important and should be opened immediately. If I had known that the sender was my commercial officer, Leslie Bracey, I would have been wary, but as it was I performed the opening in view of everyone and was highly discomfited to find that it contained nothing more urgent than a copy of *Playboy*!

The Depot Cats Rule – OK?

Railway cats were as skilled as the rest of their kind in living the good life, as Colin Driver shows.

My immediate predecessor had the foresight, and the courage, to tackle a number of costly and complicated working practices at my London goods depot.

Long-standing bonus agreements, for example, were reduced to one piece of paper as part of his streamlining efforts. One of the documents still to be revised concerned the practice of paying for food and other supplies for the depot cats.

Following the National Sundries Plan, one of the depot sheds was reopened at night. Apparently, at the time of the reopening it had been claimed there were a number of rats in the shed which needed to be killed or kept under control by the depot cats. This was countered by management's claim that during routine inspections at night, no rats had been seen. The volume of work was very light and rats would not attack staff that did not move. For these reasons, and in the light of independent advice, it was not the responsibility of management to provide food under the bonus arrangement for cats at that particular shed. The staff side's contention was that even if the original agreement was wrong, the cats could not now be left to starve by a cruel and heartless management.

My suggestion that it might be necessary to humanely drown the cats in large buckets if no food was provided by the staff themselves was viewed as a case that would have to be reported to the RSPCA! What an outrageous idea! The staff side said they understood my childhood had been spent in a quiet country vicarage – how could I be so unfeeling and cruel? (I am, in fact, an animal lover and could never hurt any animal – let alone drown it.) In the end, management got their way and the bonus clerks had one less unnecessary and time-consuming job to do. Unsurprisingly, the depot cats lived on for many years, getting even fatter due to the lack of hunting; they certainly did not starve.

Whenever I walked past the cats they were 'resting' in the shed, and I thought I could detect a slight smirk on their faces! The depot cats *still* ruled – OK?

A Royal Lift

Attendance at an official royal engagement at King's Cross produced a very special moment for Philip Benham.

The new trains delivered for the East Coast Main Line were popularised as InterCity 225s, reflecting their design speed in kilometres. Propulsion was provided by thirty-one new Class 91 electric locomotives built by British Rail Engineering Ltd at Crewe with GEC traction equipment. InterCity were keen to name these locomotives and add to the charisma of the trains. One of the names chosen was *The Red Arrows* after the celebrated aerial display team. With speed a key feature of the new electric service, such a name seemed particularly fitting.

So it was that I was required to be 'on parade' for the naming ceremony at King's Cross station of locomotive No. 91004 on 7 November 1989. The Red Arrows

were part of the RAF's Central Flying School whose commandant-in-chief was
HM Queen Elizabeth the Queen Mother, and she had agreed to perform the
naming ceremony. This was not the first such ceremony at King's Cross that year so
we were well drilled. The locomotive was positioned alongside platform 8, just inside
the northern end of the train shed. A dais was set up in front of the veiled nameplate
on the locomotive; floral decorations and red carpet were in place.

The BRB chairman, Sir Bob Reid, and I met the Queen Mother at the west side
entrance and escorted her to the platform where a number of Red Arrow pilots
formed a guard of honour. The ceremony proceeded according to plan, speeches
were made, the Queen Mother pulled back the curtains to reveal the nameplate,
and the daughter of one of the station staff presented her with flowers. The Queen
Mother was in her 90th year and, told to ensure she didn't have to walk too far,
I positioned her car on the platform to cut down the walking distance after the
ceremony. She might want to talk to the engine driver but should not be expected to
climb into the cab. Just in case, though, we had some steps in place.

Whatever the plan, the Queen Mother had her own ideas and not only wanted
to meet the driver but also to see inside his cab. A discreet hand helped her up
the steps to where John Harradine, our King's Cross traction inspector, gave a brief
explanation of the controls. Then came the interesting moment of her descent. The
Queen Mother looked at the drop, and then at me, and said with a smile, and a
twinkle in her eye, 'Young man, you had better lift me down.' And so it was that I
found myself gently lifting no less a person than Her Majesty Queen Elizabeth the
Queen Mother back on to the platform.

*Her Majesty the Queen Mother is assisted from
the locomotive cab by King's Cross area manager
Philip Benham. (Evening Standard /
Glenn Copus)*

The moment just before the lift was caught on camera for the *Evening Standard* but it was only afterwards that its significance struck me. Such familiarity in an earlier century might have meant a trip to the Tower! Twelve years later, while once again working in London, I made a journey to Whitehall. As the hearse carrying the Queen Mother's coffin passed by on its way from Westminster Abbey to Windsor, I reflected on my own special memory of this lovely royal lady.

Manchester 'Miss'-hap

When David Ward was passenger marketing manager on the LMR at Euston, a small problem provoked a lot of public complaints, one of them couched in verse.

In the early 1970s we had a great deal of trouble with one small fitting on the recently introduced Mark II carriages. When trains were in motion their vibration caused the bolts which were fitted as locks on the toilet doors to gradually work themselves loose. From inside it was possible to watch the bolt gradually undo itself and revert from the secure position to the normal one, which changed the external display back to 'vacant'.

This situation, of course, led to a number of embarrassing encounters between occupants of the loos and others who thought them to be vacant, both parties totally innocent of either lack of prudence or intention to give offence. Their discomfiture found its expression in the complaints we received, one of which was so novel that I kept a copy; the name of the writer has unfortunately been lost through time:

> To Manchester, first class, on the 8.05 fast,
> I settled in warm and unharrassed,
> Not knowing that soon I would feel like a raccoon,
> And a lady would be much embarrassed.

> I had breakfast in style and read for a while,
> 'Till nature called from afar,
> I put down my book and a short walk I took,
> To the loo at the end of the car.

> The sign on the door said 'vacant',
> So boldly I opened it wide,
> She stood their aghast, her panties half mast,
> Looking for somewhere to hide.

I retreated to the opposite corner,
Where another loo was 'vacant' once more,
I thought in a trice, 'It can't happen twice',
And proceeded to open the door.

You could see her surprise by the look in her eyes,
Not to mention the look on her face,
So I turned on my heels, you know how it feels,
And decided to wait for a sure place.

Now it seems that the vibration and motion,
Of this train when doing a ton,
Makes the bolt on the door slide open,
And the door is therefore undone.

Please, British Rail, I implore you,
Look at the bolts on this train,
It's not very nice for the ladies
And I don't want it to happen again!

The Slowest Train?

Unruly schoolchildren, watercress and a milk tank created what David Maidment thought might be BR's slowest train.

Like other management trainees in the 1950s and early '60s, I was let loose as a relief stationmaster during the last three months of training before appointment to a permanent post. In my case, I spent the early part of 1964 in Plymouth Division of the Western Region. After a freezing sojourn in Taunton as assistant yard master of an almost extinct yard, and then assistant goods agent at a depot where the local trade union officials would let no trainee on the deck of the shed (Exeter St David's), I was asked to act as stationmaster at Gillingham (Dorset) for a couple of months; this was in part of the territory the Western Region had claimed from the Southern at the beginning of the year.

No sooner was I appointed than I was asked to incorporate two further stations, Tisbury and Dinton, as the relief man there was needed somewhere else. I soon discovered that the Southern Region management had apparently ignored its non-electrified arm west of Salisbury for years and the Western had not yet fathomed what it had inherited. I believe this railway was basically operating as it had done for decades, except for the post-war influx of Bulleid Pacifics that appeared to work everything from the Atlantic Coast Express – which thundered through my station scaring the living daylights out of anyone on the platform – to the pick-up goods that I had used to deliver wage packets to the many crossing keepers on my patch because I had no other means of transport.

Among my eclectic duties was the supervision of the evening school train. We had a grammar school in the town and its boys and girls came from a fairly large rural catchment area. We ran a train for them back to Salisbury at around four o'clock, calling at Semley, Tisbury, Dinton and Wilton, arriving into Salisbury some seventy-nine minutes after departure, at the stupefying average speed of around 15mph. Was this BR's slowest scheduled train? Why did it take so long?

The four Maunsell coaches of the train would arrive from Salisbury, hauled tender first by one of the exceptions to the Bulleid rule, a Standard Class 4 Mogul. This locomotive would run round on the main line, draw the coaches back into the Up platform and then wait for the barbarian horde, pent up and released from the supervision of their draconian teachers. We were under strict instructions from a former headmistress, built, I was told, like Margaret Rutherford, to segregate the girls from the dangerous attentions of the spotty schoolboys; so we isolated the boys in the front two coaches and the girls in the rear two by locking the corridor connection in the middle of the train. In absolute contrast to the sullen crowd who crawled from the train in the morning, while I was still enjoying my breakfast in my lodgings 50yd from the station, the evening kids were exuberant. It was with great difficulty that we ever got the train away on time, after chasing the errant boys back into their own half of the train, and weeding out the odd girl who had managed to evade our scrutiny and smuggle herself into the wrong half!

And so we would set off on our raucous journey – no homework getting done in this direction. And, as I frequently accompanied the guard and our shunter, I can describe how we managed to take so long. At the first station, Semley, I would help the guard and our sole porter there to load a mountain of soggy watercress in punnets that was piled high on waiting barrows. We would sling the punnets into the brake van while the kids hung out of the windows cheering us on and making sarcastic remarks. Meanwhile, our shunter was gravitating – yes, gravitating – a loaded milk tank from the dairy private siding onto the back of the school train. I wonder if the Railway Inspectorate were ever aware of this unconventional daily movement? We were allowed fifteen minutes to accomplish this and load the watercress, which was grown in the underground storage shelters built on Salisbury Plain during the war to store essential food brought in on convoys from the United States.

Coupling accomplished and brakes tested, the locomotive would awake from its slumber and bark its way to Tisbury, where a similar mound of watercress would be awaiting us. Many of the children would scatter there, some staying to watch us frantically load the punnets, sweat pouring off us. They seemed to find this amusing. None of them ever offered to help, although had we offered a bit of pocket money, perhaps they would have obliged. So after ten minutes we would be on our way to

This 150th anniversary plaque was installed jointly by the Mayor of Gillingham and acting stationmaster David Maidment. (David Maidment)

Dinton, where we repeated the scenario. That was the end of my responsibility and I could now cross the platform and wait for a West Country-hauled three-coach local to take me back to Gillingham in time for my evening meal. Alternatively, I could go through to Salisbury and take the 17.00 Waterloo back to my on-call station at Templecombe, or go on to Yeovil Junction and spend the evening there if it was not my on-call week.

A little while ago I went back to Gillingham to celebrate the 150th anniversary of the opening of the line in that area. Class 159 diesel multiple units stop at Gillingham and Tisbury, but Semley and Dinton have now gone. I wondered how many of the people in the crowd, who were following the town band as it processed to the station to unveil the blue plaque, were once passengers on the school train. I did meet the granddaughter of my former landlady, who used to employ me to read bedtime stories to the girl while she cooked my evening meal – assuming that I hadn't been carried off by the school train to Salisbury or beyond!

I'll Be Alright

On one occasion, on a ferry crossing from Harwich to Zeebrugge, Hugh Gould came off second best in one of the captain's concerns.

As European sales manager throughout the 1970s, based at Sealink for pay and rations but with a corporate remit, I had the enviable task of visiting, and expanding, the BR network of offices in Europe. This meant over twenty trips annually, and rarely by air. Most of the journeys were made by the Harwich–Hook of Holland night service (even homeward from Paris), but interesting variations were possible and one of these, when travelling to the Brussels office, was the Harwich–Zeebrugge train ferry.

This type of poster was one of many produced to stimulate rail travel to the Continent. (National Railway Museum)

The four Eastern Region train ferries – *Norfolk Ferry*, *Suffolk Ferry*, *Cambridge Ferry* and *Essex Ferry* – with their passenger capacity of only twelve, were probably one of BR's best-kept secrets. The newest one, the *Cambridge Ferry*, was a particular joy to travel on, with side-by-side, two-berth cabins, comparable with the passenger flagship SS *Avalon*.

One evening I set out for Brussels by this route. Leaving the office at Liverpool Street at about 5.30 p.m., I caught a Norwich train to Manningtree, then the branch shuttle to Harwich Town, and so on to the train ferry by about 8 p.m. for a pleasant supper in the lounge; not perhaps the haute cuisine of the Hook route, but always very palatable. On boarding I noted two things: first, most unusually, there were several horses on the train deck in addition to the wagons; second, the weather forecast was not too kind. Nevertheless, when invited to view the departure from the bridge I accepted, as always.

We sailed sedately down past Felixstowe, but then suddenly we were in the North Sea and in worsening conditions. I recalled the advice of Sir Joseph Porter aboard HMS *Pinafore* in Gilbert and Sullivan's operetta – 'When the breezes blow I generally go below' – and decided to follow it without delay.

A minor negative feature of the *Cambridge Ferry* was that the bridge companionways were outside the hull profile, so that if you looked down while descending, you were looking straight at the North Sea. As I departed I could see the captain at the top of the stairs, looking down with a deeply concerned expression on his face. Appreciating the master's apparent anxiety for my well-being, I called, 'I'm fine! I'll be alright!' Came the reply over the gale, 'It's the horses I'm worried about!'

The Return of *Mallard*

Here, Philip Benham describes an event which he subtitles, 'The day we didn't really set fire to York station.'

Wednesday 9 July 1986 was to be a special day, when the record-breaking locomotive *Mallard* would haul a passenger train for the first time in twenty-five years.

A year or so earlier the National Railway Museum in York, supported by the Friends of the Museum, had hit on the idea of restoring the world-famous locomotive to working order ready for the fiftieth anniversary in 1988 of its record-breaking 126mph run. This was a costly exercise and the project was fortunate in securing major sponsorship from Scarborough Borough Council. The council had already paid for the installation of a turntable at Scarborough to support the Scarborough Spa Express steam trains, run each summer by British Rail because of the tourism benefit to the resort.

By the mid-1980s British Rail was rolling out sector management, with an early step being the transfer of commercial responsibilities from the regional organisations to the newly created business sectors. Special operations such as the Scarborough Spa Express now fell to the new InterCity sector, which in early 1986 made it clear that, after mixed financial results the previous year, they did not want to continue with the service. Not surprisingly, given their commitment to the *Mallard* project, this caused some consternation at Scarborough. The council chairman demanded a meeting with the InterCity business manager in York, Simon Fraser. As the local area manager I was called in to give moral support. The council were very persuasive and Simon, a reasonable and politically shrewd man, listened carefully. His problem was that, faced with the challenges of the East Coast Main Line in the early throes of electrification, his small team could not spare the time for such a peripheral operation. The meeting dragged on; then in a sudden about-turn, Simon looked at me and said, 'My staff haven't got the time, you will have to do it' – and so it was agreed.

True, there was a lot to organise, but we already provided the crew, arranged servicing for the engines and operated the trains. Marketing was the major new task which my area passenger manager, Stuart Baker, and travel centre manager, Ron Fisher, and their team took to with enthusiasm. I was also charged with keeping accounts for the operation, and for ensuring the trains covered their costs. Finally, there was the need to negotiate for suitable engines to run the service, since the days when BR had its own steam engines were long gone. This is where we come back to *Mallard*.

Given Scarborough Council's commitment to *Mallard*'s restoration, the engine was the obvious choice to launch the reprieved 1986 Scarborough Spa Express season. For such a historic event, however, something distinctive was needed. So we arranged for *Mallard* to run on a special circular itinerary from York to Scarborough, down the Wolds Coast line, around Hull via Anlaby Curve, on to Selby and back down the East Coast Main Line to York.

Wednesday 9 July dawned fine and sunny. *Mallard* had successfully completed a main-line test run to Scarborough and Doncaster some time before, and all was set. The return to steam of such a famous engine had attracted considerable public interest, and both of Yorkshire's regional TV stations were sending crews to cover the event. In plenty of time to ensure a prompt departure, driver Harry Wilson had drawn *Mallard* and its train of Mark I coaches alongside the south end of York station's platform 9 under the famous roof. This was looking particularly resplendent after a major facelift of the timber cladding.

All was going well; hundreds of cameras were clicking, while passengers and onlookers crowded admiringly round the engine, ladies in their summer finery,

and others in lightly coloured clothing reflecting the warm, sunny weather. BBC Look North, whose camera crew were to accompany the train, asked me if it would be possible to arrange a 'dummy departure' for them to film. 'Of course,' said I, as this could easily be done by drawing the train forward from the south to the north end of the long platform.

Station staff closed the doors, the train announcer warned everyone to stand clear, the guard gave the tip

Shrouding the scene in steam and smoke, world record-breaking Pacific locomotive Mallard *is celebrating its return to steam by adding a little unsolicited soot to York station's roof and passengers. (Philip Benham)*

and Harry opened *Mallard's* regulator. LNER Pacifics were always prone to wheel slip, especially starting from the curved platform 9 at York. And so it proved for the old girl faced with moving a heavy train for the first time in over twenty years. It was only a little slip, which Harry quickly had under control, but it was enough to send a column of sooty smoke vertically up to the roof before cascading down onto the unsuspecting crowds. Standing with the film crew on the opposite platform, my white shirt was covered with sooty deposits, and so, unfortunately, was the clothing of many others. With the departure time now approaching, I quickly shepherded the camera team aboard the train, and through the rest of what was a very successful day the incident was soon forgotten.

Remarkably, I cannot recall BR receiving any public complaints, or demands for compensation for soiled clothing. There was to be a sequel, however. Brian Davis, Eastern Region's chief civil engineer, was understandably less than amused at the effect of the smoky outburst on his roof, where a large black stain now stood out against the white timber cladding. I was told this would cost around £8,000 to clean, and was instructed to debit this against the costs of the Scarborough Spa Express operation. Despite this, come the end of the season we still declared a healthy profit of £35,000 from the trains, enough to persuade InterCity to run them again the following year.

In fact, the cleaning was never done, with the stain remaining in situ until the next refurbishment of York station roof in recent years by Network Rail. Almost twenty years later, commuting daily from York to King's Cross, I could look up at the black-stained roof and recall with a wry smile the day we didn't actually set fire to York station.

Expresso Supper

Railway passengers have long proved adept at customising their journeys; that this is not a modern phenomenon is clear from a story handed down in Graham Paterson's family.

In 1965 my great-aunt recorded this story about her father. Apparently he was 'someone in the City' and returned nightly to the family home in Birchington on the Kent coastline. He often changed his homeward plans at short notice and one night, when he had to attend a last-minute meeting at Margate, he took the Granville Express which did not stop at Birchington.

Before leaving London, he sent a sixpenny telegram informing his family that he would pick up some fish and throw it from the train window at a particular spot just before Birchington. The neat objective was that by the time he got home after the meeting, the fish would have been retrieved, cooked and on the table. In a rising wind, mistress and maid set out for the rendezvous – but no package emerged from the windows of the passing express. The man returned to a fishless home and insisted on a further search to prove he had done his part. A track search in the dark eventually revealed most of the fish, flesh and fowl that had been in the package, strewn along the line-side hedgerow, and it was duly recovered – not greatly the worse for its unconventional delivery.

Later it became clear that the throw had been mistimed and the straw bag in which it had been packed had struck a telegraph pole and burst open. Perhaps this was a mercy, for had it landed on the waiting wife, it would, to say the least, have spoiled her hat!

Interestingly, Geoff Body recalls that in his early journeys home from Finsbury Park to Sandy in Bedfordshire he had a not dissimilar 'early warning' arrangement. Newly married and in a rented house a couple of fields from the East Coast Main Line his train was clearly visible to his watching wife. This sighting was sufficient supper notice in daylight hours, but to identify the train in darkness the compartment light was used: short flashes for 'home in twenty minutes' and long ones for 'on the Slow Road waiting for an express to pass before we can be let out on to the Main and into Sandy platform'. Mostly it worked.

Special Workings

Being in charge of a variety of special workings gave Philip Benham a taste of both the pleasant and the unpleasant.

One of the more interesting aspects of being a divisional inspector was accompanying special workings of one sort or another. I once spent a leisurely day trundling up the Midland Main Line from Derby with a new type of German self-propelled, on-track machine being trialled by the Rail Research Centre. All went well until we passed from the remotely signalled power box area into manual signal box land south of Loughborough, where we were promptly stopped at a signal. The signalman had sent the bell code 'stop and examine' because although we were displaying two red electric lights at the rear in good German railway practice, his understanding of the rulebook was that we should have a good old traditional British oil-lit tail lamp!

Particularly enjoyable assignments were the inspection tours run for the Nottingham divisional civil and signalling engineers. These involved the use of a specially built saloon coach, comfortably equipped and fitted with large panoramic windows at each end. The engineers sat up front inspecting the line ahead while the saloon was propelled along. A lever operated a warning bell, and a series of bell codes allowed communication with the driver. There was no guard; as divisional inspector in charge this was my role and included working the retractable steps down to track level, operated through the vacuum brake.

The Nottingham Division covered much of the East Midlands coalfields, together with more rural parts from a northern boundary touching on the Peak District, and south almost to Bedford. The saloon inspections, often traversing rarely visited colliery and freight branches, were an effective way of covering the territory and planning future maintenance and track renewals. Nowadays, most of this work is done by the modern gadgetry of track-recording trains.

A Special Traffic Notice, setting out timings, would be issued to signal boxes, stations and depots in advance. Saloon tours were designated as Class 1, which gave them the same priority as an express passenger train (later downgraded to Class 2, the equivalent of an ordinary passenger train). A lunch stop was always scheduled, the saloon having its own kitchen and chef, whose day job was as the divisional engineer's chauffeur. Beer and wines were available in those days, before alcohol was banned, and, incredible as it may seem now, one of my jobs as inspector was to take a couple of bottles of beer to the driver and his second man on their Sulzer Type 2 locomotive.

Another important duty, though not quite so pleasant, was accompanying the weedkiller train which covered all routes each spring during the prime weed-growing period. Chipman's No. 2 Weedkilling Train was made up from old Southern Railway passenger coaches with a couple of tank wagons for the weedkiller solution. This was mixed up to the required strength in a large tub in one of the coaches by the contractor, whose staff seemed immune to the vile dust that got everywhere. Sprays on the end coach directed the solution on to the track and adjoining formation. Once again, the inspector performed the guard's role. An essential task was to guide the weedkilling staff on where, or more particularly where not, to spray. In a previous year, British Railways had been obliged to pay compensation after the train had neatly sprayed the back gardens of several houses alongside the Trowell line in one of Nottingham's more fashionable suburbs!

Such trains still run, but I am told that the weedkiller potions of yesteryear are now banned substances. This partly explains why modern railways often seem plagued by weeds, and could account for why I always seemed to have a sore after travelling with this train.

Interviews

During a thirty-year career with BR and Transmark, David Jagoe, surprisingly, only ever had two formal job interviews.

The first of these was in Cardiff when I responded to an advertisement in the *Daily Telegraph* for a field sales manager, part of Lord Beeching's move to transfuse fresh marketing blood into BR. The interview took place in the divisional manager's office, which I later learned was known as The Trough because of an old wooden plaque on top of the bookcase reading, 'This Water Trough is for the Use of Western Region Horses Only'. I was appointed, which infuriated divisional manager Bob Hilton who was away at the time, although I did subsequently make peace with this remarkable railwayman.

I began my new career on 1 April 1967 – a propitious date? Promotion later followed to divisional marketing and sales manager, responsible for the commercial aspects of the considerable freight and passenger business in South Wales. Then, in 1971, I was summoned to attend what turned out to be a most bizarre interview at BRB headquarters, where a number of marketing roles were to be filled.

The board interview was conducted by Willie Thorpe, the deputy chairman, along with Stanley Robbins and Tony Griffiths, the board members for freight and passenger traffic respectively. I was invited to take a seat at the far end of a long and very grand table and W.T. opened the proceedings by explaining that I had worked in the past in my family business of agri-horticultural and building suppliers, and if anyone had any gardening questions they should seek my advice. There followed a lengthy discussion about a problem W.T. was having with his lawn and we then moved on to black spot on his roses. At this point W.T. went off to the toilet, inviting the other two to carry on with the interview. They asked a few desultory general questions and I was then sent back to Cardiff.

In the event, I was appointed as the marketing manager for petroleum and chemicals, which led on to a number of other senior appointments on the freight side of the business. I worked with some very able people but admit that I learned little from that initial interview.

On the LT&S

Basil Tellwright was among a small but dedicated group running the LT&S line in its early days, and remembers some incidents from its busy daily pattern of traffic.

A Bit of Prestige

The LT&S line in the 1960s was a proud, and maybe slightly arrogant, undertaking due to its manageable size, complex activities and revenue-earning capacity. Under the able direction of its movements and maintenance people, including Bob Arnott, Jim Urquhart, Geoff Parslew and the imperturbable Frank Southgate, it not only moved a lot of passenger and freight trains each day, but also undertook some major changes. The headquarters at Saracen's House, conveniently near Fenchurch Street station, had a lively commercial team led by Ted Taylor and Geoff Foulger. They built up the traffic to impressive levels, especially the flows to and from Fords at Dagenham, block trainloads of oil and cement from Grays and Thames Haven, docks traffic from riverside wharves between Poplar and Purfleet, and passenger usage over the whole length of the line. Stan Eccles was the staff manager and public relations officer Percy Gillett maintained the line's image.

One complex job was the replacement of the first diesel locomotives – the D61xx series of Type 2 engines built by the North British company – with the infinitely superior Brush Type 2s (later Class 31/0) numbers D5500–19. This enabled the line to develop the full through train working of its important oil and cement traffic. Thanks to an exhaustive pattern of route learning with the new fleet, we were able to operate out and back to a number of oil and cement terminals where a loaded train was left and the empties worked back with the same locomotive and men. This was very popular, for at last the LT&S men saw more of the world than Acton, Willesden and Cricklewood.

On one particular afternoon I had a call from the control office asking for someone to speak to Euston Control. At the time we had a daily out and back cement train from Grays to Tring. Euston had asked our Ripple Lane driver to surrender his locomotive so that it could be used to take over the Up Royal Scot which had failed at Tring. The LT&S driver had refused but had offered to work the failed train with his own engine and then return to complete his working back to Grays. I backed him up. A bit proud and arrogant, perhaps, but our men knew the way from Camden to Birmingham and it was not such an outrageous suggestion. The Brush might have struggled a bit but it is mostly downhill from Tring.

Getting On with the Job

On one of those rare quiet days I was given the task of examining the passenger guards' journals for the previous day. It was a tedious job but, if done thoroughly, gave quite a lot of data on the loading of passenger trains in terms of people and parcels. Delays could be investigated and action taken to improve performance. The LT&S Line operated on a 'time means time' policy, i.e. the journal entry 'time' should mean exactly on time and not within five minutes either way. The task was very important.

On this particular day the guard of the 14.40 ex Fenchurch Street had recorded in his journal, '20 minutes Purfleet Rifle Range (signal box) waiting acceptance Purfleet'. The control office log showed no delay at all for this service. An enquiry to the station manager brought the question, 'How did you know about that?' And when told of the guard's journal record, his response was '***** idiot', or words to that effect. On being pressed for an explanation of what had really happened, the station manager said that a WD locomotive had been derailed 'all wheels' on the trailing crossover in the station. They had seen it come off and decided to try to reverse it back on again with the help of some permanent way men. I said that he had taken a big risk, but he observed, 'It was already off and couldn't be more off, so it was worth a try.' I put the journal back in the pile!

Not Suitable

One morning, a driver and mate booked on at Tilbury shed to work an end of peak passenger train set to run all stations to Barking; it was to run around there, then all stations back to Tilbury Riverside, shunt the stock away and remain to work 'as required' until the end of their shift. The driver was offered one of the original 4-4-2 tank engines for the job but after inspection declared it unsuitable. He was then offered one of the newer ex-LMS 2-6-4 tanks, but this, too, did not find favour. When the shed running foreman said that he had nothing else to offer, the response was, 'I'll take that one', pointing to an Immingham Britannia which had come in overnight on the regular Fisons chemical train to Thames Haven. So he did, and at the end of his day revealed that it was his last working day and he had always wanted to drive a Pacific!

Ruffled Feathers

On a rather damp afternoon, one of Ripple Lane's Class 31s, with forty-five loaded coal wagons, was taking an Acton to Ripple Lane trip over the Tottenham & Hampstead Joint Line. The driver had the South Tottenham Down Distant signal against him and started braking. When he came under the bridge below the Enfield line he realised that he was not holding the heavy load and was likely to overrun the Inner Home. At the same time he was startled to see an officers' special with the Great Eastern line manager's saloon coming round the curve from Seven Sisters, and was even more startled to see it come to a stand in the station. The coal train continued to slow, and finally came gently to a stop 'buffered up' to the saloon.

The occupants of the saloon were civic dignitaries being shown round the GE electrification by Harold Few, the Liverpool Street traffic manager. Seeing the approaching coal train they started abandoning ship. The area manager, who happened to be on the platform at the time, commented at the subsequent internal inquiry that 'he had never seen top brass move so quickly'. Mr Few was off the saloon in a flash, over the footbridge and on the phone to Fenchurch Street demanding to speak to the LT&S line manager to register his strong protest.

An internal inquiry was held but as no one was injured, apart from their pride, and a passenger train was not involved, the incident did not have to be reported to the Railway Inspectorate. The resulting recommendation was that the LT&S Freight Trains Load book should be brought into line with the GE version which had a limit of thirty-nine coal wagons on similar trains.

A Thirty-Two-Coach Train

Soon after the introduction of the full electric service on the LT&S, a twelve-coach train, made up of three four-car Class 302 units, failed on the notorious Chalkwell Bank approaching Southend Central. The train behind was an eight-car train and, after the due safety arrangements had been carried out, this was brought up behind the failed train to assist. Unfortunately, the driver of the relieving train joined the two together with the electric 'jumper' leads. Now we had two failed trains.

The third train to come along was a twelve-car set so this was brought up and the brakes coupled, but *not* the electrics! The long procession, now thirty-two

vehicles in all and full of Down peak period passengers, set off to call at all stations to Shoeburyness. This raised a few eyebrows on the way but was achieved successfully. Unfortunately, the disruption meant that the failed trains were not available for the Up peak services, so some incoming trains had to be reversed at Leigh-on-Sea. However, Southend's alternative station at Victoria got an unexpected traffic bonus.

Electrification in 1962 transformed the LT&S line and finally wiped away time-honoured locations like the locomotive depot at Plaistow, which had kept its worn-out steam locomotives working right up to the changeover moment.

J.W. Dedman

'JWD', our line manager, was a martinet, expecting much in dedication and achievement. Yet he commanded immense respect. I got rebuked for taking additional people to a meeting at Dagenham East involving the transfer of the District Line operations from BR to London Transport. I was told to find out all I needed and not 'take half the office with me'! I never forgot this directive. But JWD was a fair and inspirational man under whose leadership the hotchpotch of influences which had been the LT&S became a successful unit: it electrified the line from end to end, built three new panel boxes, a new station at Barking with two flyovers and a dive-under, and successfully introduced a complete new marshalling yard and goods depot complex at Ripple Lane.

It may be a measure of JWD that when he was at Cambridge the control office rang his home one evening to report a split buckeye coupling on the Down Fenman. Mrs Dedman answered and was asked to take a message, the controller clearly expecting to have to explain what a buckeye coupling was. She responded by saying, in no uncertain terms, 'If you'd been married to JW as long as I have, you would certainly know all there is to know about a buckeye!'

Show Me the Way to Go Home

Informing the public about changes to services is vital, but Alex Bryce came across a couple of pitfalls at Waterloo and Clapham Junction.

As assistant divisional manager, South Western Division, Wimbledon, one of my tasks was dealing with public relations and complaints. With the divisional manager, then Llew Edwards, one of our first daily jobs was to scrutinise the morning mail and identify and react to any highly critical complaints that might demand urgent attention. On one occasion an unofficial 'go slow' by drivers had caused quite serious disruption to evening peak services and predictably, the incoming mail contained a range of complaints from irate commuters. There was one particular complaint that caught our attention as it referred, unusually, to the piped music that in those days was played over the terminal's public address system at Waterloo. This was designed to encourage and indeed motivate the commuter flows at peak morning arrival and evening departure times of the day.

The complainant heavily criticised the selection of music being played at certain times; on a very bad night, when evening services were cancelled and seriously disrupted, he alleged that the piped music included the words *Show me the way to go home – I'm tired and I wanna go to bed*. It was easy to imagine how provocative and indeed offensive this could be to an individual whose evening service had been badly disrupted.

As a result of this complaint, we reviewed the arrangements for the playing of such music and in particular the pieces played and by whom, as it was clear the train announcer could not be solely responsible for what came over the public address system. It was never confirmed, however, that the particular piece that had given rise to the complaint had ever been played, and it was not among the normal selection available. It appeared to be a practical joke, but we were never sure who was involved.

We were engaged at this time in improving the quality of our on-train and station announcements, and the advice to passengers in notices displayed when train services were delayed or cancelled. It was clearly appreciated by travellers when services were disrupted. For example, on Monday mornings after a heavy programme of weekend engineering works, timely advice and early warnings could greatly facilitate alternative arrangements. But, despite all the good work, there were inevitably occasions when we did not quite get it right.

Special blackboard notices were on display one morning at Clapham Junction as I travelled from Wimbledon to Waterloo. There had been signalling problems and the wording with appropriate apologies referred to services being delayed owing to *intermitant* track failures. On reaching Waterloo I arranged for the supervisor there to correct the misspelling. Back at Wimbledon, later that day, I was astonished to see that the notice had been altered with the misspelling *intermitant* changed to another misspelling, *intermitent*. I therefore arranged for our control office to again advise Clapham Junction to correct this further error as the signalling faults sadly continued to affect us.

The following morning I had again reason to visit Waterloo and on arrival at Clapham Junction decided to check that the error had now been put right. It was with some wry amusement that I found the notice had again been altered, but this time to read that the services were delayed owing to *spasmodic* signalling problems. As it happened, the faults were put right that morning and this particular problem was at last satisfactorily resolved.

Lured by a Bird

Philip Benham believes that Margaret Thatcher may have developed a higher opinion of BR as a result of her encounters at King's Cross.

During her long period as prime minister, Margaret Thatcher was renowned for her aversion to rail travel. Yet while I was area manager at King's Cross there were three occasions when we were able to persuade her to put aside her antipathy.

The first occurred on 7 February 1987 for a ceremony to mark the 'planting' at York station of the first overhead mast as part of the East Coast Main Line electrification. The plan was for the prime minister to travel on the 08.00 from King's Cross in the executive saloon – a Mark III coach specially fitted out for corporate entertaining that could be marshalled within a standard High Speed Train set. Once at York, she would take part in the ceremony, including unveiling a plaque on the mast and visiting the National Railway Museum.

Within the senior circles of British Rail, there was some apprehension as to what would happen if something went wrong, such as a train failure. Quite apart from the embarrassment, the Troubles in Northern Ireland were at their height and there were security issues to consider. So a contingency plan was hatched with the regional operations manager, Colin McKeever, for a duplicate train to shadow the 08.00 from King's Cross some ten minutes later, as a back-up. This in itself caused some anxiety to the BRB deputy chairman, David Kirby, who was fearful that if this plan leaked out to the press, BR would be lampooned for the expense and lack of confidence in its own trains. So we needed a cover story. By good fortune, InterCity were holding a promotion for the Family Railcard, giving free travel if children were carrying a teddy bear. 'Expecting large numbers of extra passengers because of the teddy bear promotion, a relief train has been laid on to avoid overcrowding' – at least that was what we told the deputy chairman, and who could say we were being anything other than prudent! In the event, all went well and the PM was said to be charmed.

The subsequent occasions were altogether more local affairs for the King's Cross area. The Royal Society for the Protection of Birds has its headquarters very close to the East Coast Main Line at Sandy, and 1989 was its centenary year. To mark the anniversary, BR had agreed to name an engine *Avocet*, the official symbol of the society. With East Coast electrification well under way, the RSPB had initially been offered the first of the new Class 91 '225' electric locomotives, but the Class 91s were still under test and for various technical reasons were deemed unsuitable. Consideration was given briefly to a Class 90, then coming into service on the West Coast Main Line, before the happy choice of No. 89001 was made. This was the first electric locomotive delivered for East Coast service. It had become a regular on our King's Cross to Peterborough commuter trains, thus passing the RSPB site daily, and in the area and at Bounds Green depot we regarded it very much as 'our' engine.

An invitation by the RSPB president, Magnus Magnusson, was enough to persuade the prime minister to perform the naming ceremony at King's Cross on 16 January 1989. The event would also mark the issue by the Post Office of a set of commemorative bird stamps.

From the moment Mrs Thatcher got out of the prime ministerial car there was no doubt she was in charge and the visit progressed to her agenda. Accompanied by the RSPB president, Sir Brian Nicholson, the chairman of the Post Office and the British Railways chairman – the first Sir Bob Reid – we attempted to escort her to platform 8 for the naming, although more precisely she led the way. The ceremony proceeded without a hitch, and then it was over to me to introduce Mrs Thatcher to the special train driver, John Hopwood. A picture of John with the

After its naming by Margaret Thatcher at King's Cross, Avocet *arrives at Sandy with its special train. Behind, the original station buildings contrast with a modern silo. (Philip Benham)*

prime minister later appeared on the front page of *Rail News* and he received a copy of the photograph signed by the lady herself. John took some ribbing from his more socialist-minded colleagues at King's Cross depot for being seen alongside such a controversial Conservative figure, but of course he was only doing his job and affording the respect due to any dignitary, not least the prime minister of the day.

Then it was off to Sandy with the newly named locomotive heading the train. Sadly, the prime minister left by road immediately after the naming ceremony, thus missing the chance of another prime ministerial train journey. But there was to be a sequel. Mrs T was persuaded to pay another visit to the RSPB Sandy headquarters some months later. Furthermore, she would travel there by train.

So it was that on Thursday 31 August 1989, *Avocet*, of course, whisked the prime minister and a trainload of invited guests on the short 37-mile journey from King's Cross to Sandy. This was an altogether more informal affair and I was entrusted to front it for BR, although my boss, Bill Robinson, the regional operations manager, was keeping a weather eye open as officer in charge on the train. John Cronin and his team at Bounds Green depot had done their customary fine job in turning out the short coaching set in 'white wall' condition, the engine performed faultlessly and the day was a great success.

None Shall Sleep

David Crathorn's experiences at Cricklewood ranged from bed bugs to complex workings.

I had been the stationmaster/goods agent at Cricklewood for a few months and had just got used to the peculiarities of the patch when the telephone rang in our flat just after midnight. Control told me that the relatively young district relief signalman at Acton Canal Wharf signal box had been taken ill. I had an old Ford van and was soon driving down Willesden Lane to the Chesebrough Pond's factory. BR had sold a parcel of land for building the factory and there was no route from the highway to reach the signal box; you had to go to the factory gates and get the gatekeeper to let you through from the road and then ask him to open the far gate to access the track.

When I reached the box the signalman was lying down on the bench seat and his left leg was greatly swollen. With commendable speed, the ambulance men appeared with a stretcher, having come through the factory, too. Due to the unusual circumstance, the public health officer for the borough concerned was alerted. I stayed and worked the signal box until the relief man arrived at 06.00. It felt pretty lonely, but the other signalmen at Acton Wells Junction and Neasden Midland Junction were helpful.

I went home for breakfast and arranged to meet the public health man on site at 09.00. I conducted him through the factory, we entered the signal box and the relieving signalman stood aside. After a short while the public health man looked up and said, 'Who sleeps in here?' I explained that no one should, although relief men were known for their inventive arrangements. Apparently, the hospital had reported that our man had suffered an allergic reaction to bed bug bites. The life of the bed bug, which can be carried into premises on clothing or in a bag or blanket, is simple. It climbs up the wall and across the ceiling until it senses heat rising from a recumbent body beneath. It then drops on to the exposed flesh and draws its fill of blood. In most cases, the person or animal does not suffer ill effects.

In the summer of 1966, this Acton Canal Wharf location became very busy. BR wanted slick, modern trains to join Euston to Wembley Stadium to convey VIPs going to the World Cup events. Rolls-Royce-powered four-car diesel multiple units were used and ran Fast Line from Euston to Willesden No. 7 signal box. There they reversed smartly and proceeded via the single-track connecting line to Acton Canal Wharf. After another reversal they accelerated up the hill, over the West Coast Main Line to Neasden Midland Junction, where they diverted left down on to the Great Central and then immediately right into Stadium station. It was an impressive operation.

Ne Worry Pas

During a temporary period with Eurostar, Jim Gibbons found his limitations with the French language gently mocked in a spoof 'transcript' circulated by his colleagues.

Dans les offices des supervisors de depot Bounds Green et Lyons une nuit en 1994:

Voice 1   Bonjour. C'est Lyon Depot de Maintenance speaking. Nous avons une problem avec un 142.

Voice 2   Un 142. Qu'est-ce qu'un 142 doing a Lyon? Je thought 142 couldn't traverse le tunnel de Channel. A cause de fumer du exhauste.

Voice 1   Oui, c'est true. Mais l'AOC de Leeds exchange un 142 pour un TGV qui a window casse par un vandal avec un brique a Neville Hill. First indication a nous was quand le 12.16 de Wakefield a Marseille a ete longue time in en section entre Calais et Amiens. Le line speed y-est 300km/h; plus quick je think, pour un 142 avec engine reverant au idle.

Voice 2   Et now, ou est le 142 avec le trouble?

Voice 1   Ici, a notre depot de maintenance. Il est limped in hier au roz de running repairs.

Voice 2   Sacre bleu! Nous avons enough difficulte getting les units HST back de depot de Heaton, never mind 142 a Lyons!

Voice 1   Ne worry pas. Ici nous avons un mechanique qui a eu peut experience au 'space shuttle'. Perhaps nous could reperer le unit, mais il sera necessaire que vous FAX a nous un schematique du systems electrique power controls.

Voice 2   Oui, ca c'est une bonne idée. Mais etes-vous certifies de Eurostandard ISO 9000?

Voice 1   Naturellement.

Voice 2   Bon. Il est necessaire de check ca. Et je vous send aussi un transistor panel juste-en-cas.

Voice 1   Oui, bon thinking – par le service de Red Star Parcels?

Voice 2   Oui, certainement. Je don't know how to thank vous. Vous aurait eu beaucoup de trouble.

Voice 1   Oh, think nothing de ca. Mais peut etre vous could slip un kilo de Jellied Eels de East End into le parcel. Je suis un connoisseur.

Voice 2   OK. Je le ferais. Merci again Lyon, et bon chance.

Beaujolais Nouveau

Jim Gibbons remembers an advertising promotion that went seriously awry.

Area managers of London stations had to accept the commercial promotional activity that was arranged by higher authorities. Businesses were keen to offer their goods and services to the widest possible audience, and what better place to do so than a London station concourse in the peak hours?

The race to be the first to bring in the season's Beaujolais to the UK by the most bizarre mode of transport has now all but disappeared, but years ago it was an annual event well covered by the media. In the year in question all stations were advised that a well-known wine merchant concern would be on our stations at Beaujolais Nouveau time dispensing glasses of the said wine. On the appointed day the promotion people arrived with a trestle table, glasses, several cases of wine and two very lovely ladies dressed in tight trousers, black-and-white striped T-shirts and saucy berets. Unfortunately, the area around one of my stations was renowned for its, shall we say, earthy residents. When the word got round that alcohol had appeared and was being dispensed gratis, the jungle drums went into overdrive and the said residents arrived en masse, like a locust storm. They relieved the lovely ladies of their bottles on their way through and disappeared within a few minutes, leaving just the table and glasses and nothing to put in them!

Crushing Experience

The start of a major freight traffic flow also provided a minor shock for Geoff Body.

In August 1970 BRB chairman Sir Henry Johnson visited the Foster Yeoman Torr Works at Merehead in Somerset to celebrate the opening of a new railway freight facility with John Yeoman. Crushed Mendip limestone was already being despatched from the firm's Dulcote quarry, although the new plant and rail link at Merehead would not only provide significant block trainload forwardings, but would grow to the point where the firm operated its own destination terminals, wagons and locomotives.

Along with Peter Nicholls, my stone project manager, and other BR staff, I was present on this auspicious occasion when the naming of a locomotive, *Western Yeoman*, was followed by a tour of the works. This included the crushing plant where large blocks of stone were reduced to small pieces by brute compression.

The size and extent of the new Foster Yeoman quarry railhead is clear from this 1970 view of its opening and first block trainload of stone.

Despite my contact with other heavy industries, nothing had prepared me for the experience of looking down upon the crusher in action. It was primeval, the stone splitting with more and more vivid red sparks and deafening cracks, tectonics in action! For a few seconds I felt that normality had been suspended and the rail of the viewing platform was my only reassurance.

Back to normal and I noticed that the Yeoman people were grinning – in that non-malicious way I had seen on the face of the winder when I made my first cage descent at Tilmanstone Colliery!

Belle Finale

Frank Paterson had to decide on and oversee the fate of the much-loved Brighton Belle Pullman.

I was appointed divisional manager for Central in April 1970 and the furore following the removal of kippers from the breakfast menu on the Brighton Belle was still fresh in my mind. So very early on I thought I'd better get acquainted with the train. The cab was incredibly cramped for space and the driver's seat was hinged to the door so that he had to stand up to let anybody join him. We had a fairly militant drivers' local departmental committee at Brighton and they kept pressing for some improvements; they were not fans of the Belle. The interior of the carriages looked a bit tired but still had the distinctive, pleasant Pullman ambience. The stewards were great; all had a certain style about them and this, of course, paid handsome dividends. The journey – 51 miles in sixty minutes – was leisurely, but the ride was dreadful.

I asked the chief mechanical engineer, Maurice Maguire, for a price for refurbishing. I can't recall now what it was but there was certainly no business case for the investment. Although it was a luxury train, the passengers were not paying luxury prices to cover the high on-train staffing costs. The inescapable conclusion was that there was no longer justification for a freestanding Pullman service between London and Brighton. Lance Ibbotson was general manager and gave his full backing, but said he was not going to be involved and the inevitable hostile reactions had to be dealt with in the division.

The responses were predictable: public totally anti, drivers quite happy. The revenue and expenditure figures were seldom disputed so most of the arguments were on heritage and emotion. And there was a lot of emotion. An effigy of me was hung on the platform at Brighton by one group. But the theatricals were the most vocal. Many of the big names in theatre lived in Brighton and used the last Belle to get home. But two or three gins and a Welsh rarebit was all they needed after the show and that didn't help the bottom line.

The Mayor of Brighton at that time was a successful property developer and I remember my wife Grace and I being invited to a dinner with him and a few friends at his palatial house. His 'friends' were all users of the Belle, including Laurence Olivier and John Clements. After a pleasant meal the men moved to the library and Olivier delivered a prepared speech, standing with his back to the blazing fire in a magnificent book-lined room, appealing for a stay of execution. The oratory was memorable but the saddest thing to me was that he kept referring to his notes!

The last day of Belle operations was Sunday 30 April 1972 and, despite premium fares, we had full loadings on every trip. The last Up train from Brighton featured a wine and cheese party and I still have the menu for the final run at 22.30 from Victoria, viz:

Pate Maison, Demi-Poussin & Ham, Mixed and Russian Salad, Sherry Trifle, Champagne Mercier Private Brut, Merrydown Mead. The Bar Tariff: Tio Pepe – 22p, Whisky 'Royal Scot' – 37p, Gin – 37p.

We had invited as guests a lot of the celebrity season ticket holders and I remember particularly Dame Flora Robson, Moira Lister, Dora Bryan and Jimmy Edwards – Olivier declined saying there was nothing to celebrate. The platform at Victoria had a brass band and spontaneous dancing, and was crowded despite the fact that we charged £1 to get on. BBC Radio had a studio on the train and Pete Murray interviewed the celebrities, passengers and railway staff. Two incidents come to mind:

I was talking with Jimmy Edwards while he was eating and Pete Murray sent a message asking him to join him in the studio. I apologised for the interruption and he retorted in his gravelly voice, 'I'd be happy to be interrupted anywhere for two minutes on the air!'

Ron Neills was area manager at Victoria and in the course of his interview mentioned that his wife had had to call off because their daughter had chicken pox. The following week, when Harold Wilson was being escorted by Ron to his train, the prime minister asked, 'And how is your daughter?' How's that for being well briefed?

At Brighton there was another band greeting the Belle's arrival and an open-top bus showing off our celebrity cargo to the thousands of people who had gathered on the approaches to the station. It was a fitting climax to a memorable day and a great send-off for an iconic legend.

And here is a final quote from the souvenir menu:

> Today is the end of an era
> The final chapter in an unforgettable episode of railway history
> The last run of the Brighton Belle
> It's goodbye to Hazel, Doris, Audrey, Vera, Gwen and Mona.
> And their frilly lamp shades and old-world charm
> It's a sad day. We will miss them.
> But one can't survive on nostalgia
> Let us remember them fondly but realistically
> As ladies in retirement.

Saloons & Me

Inspection saloons played an important working role on railways from their beginnings, linking the operational activity with those who managed it. They were also a fine vehicle not only for observing the work, but for enjoying the experience, as 'railwayman' the Hon. Sir William McAlpine records.

David Ward gave me *Signal Box Coming Up, Sir!* I read it and thoroughly enjoyed it. My expression of this brought a request from Bill Parker to make a contribution to the next volume. I rashly said yes, but what to write? Although I have had a life-long interest in railways, I have never worked directly for the railway. I have, however, served on two advisory boards when they were in use by British Railways, both the Southern Region and the Western. I also currently chair two independent railways, the Dart Valley and the Romney, Hythe & Dymchurch, and have the honour of chairing the Railway Heritage Trust which, financed by Network Rail, gives grants to improve and restore network structures of all sorts. I was once much pleased when someone introduced me as a 'railwayman' when naming a locomotive; but what to write with no operational experiences to draw on? I decided that I had to find something that was unique. I came up with the Chairman's Special, when I was able to entertain on my own special train the then chairman of BR and all the living chairmen of the British Transport Commission and BR.

First I must explain how this came about. My father used to give an annual cocktail party for family members to entertain their clients and friends. There would be among the guests senior railwaymen, and on one occasion Sir Peter Parker was there. He was a great man and a tremendous wit. He was interviewed on the BBC Today programme and revealed that the BR breakfast (a blessed memory) was more expensive than the Savoy. 'But the Savoy doesn't go anywhere,' said he. At the party he started surmising what the collective noun was for chairmen: a Board of Chairmen, a Deficit, a Pride, a Cascade, a Sitting, a Sedan, a Gavel …?

I had the idea to entertain the ex-chairmen on a trip around London. I had organised such an excursion to entertain our clients. So the day before this trip, I had invited Sir John Elliott (chairman from 1951–53), Lord Beeching (1961–65), Sir Stanley Raymond (1965–67), Lord Marsh (1971–76) and Sir Bob Reid (1990–95), sadly all now deceased, and to my surprise and delight they all accepted. With my father, we all set off from Marylebone on 4 May 1984. For a reason that I have to explain later, we stopped for forty minutes at Clapham Junction in silence. The old coaches were much noisier than they are today but we were able to talk easily while eating roast beef and drinking claret!

BR chairmen pictured in 1984. In the back row, from left to right, are Lord Marsh, Sir Stanley Raymond, Lord McAlpine of Moffat, Sir Peter Parker, Lord Beeching, Robert Reid and Sir William McAlpine; in the front row are Sir Henry Johnson and Sir John Elliot. (Sir William McAlpine)

It was absolutely fascinating to hear each talk of his time as chairman. It seemed to be a common opinion that it was a marvellous job, but the main drawback was satisfying the Minister of Transport and his civil servants. There was some competition as to who had the most ministers as they varied from two to seven. But what an experience, truly it was, listening to recent railway history from the top. Eventually we moved off and continued our circular tour to Marylebone. I enquired about the reason for the happy delay, to be told that the guard allocated was not passed for the route and wouldn't take the train out. Fortunately, his chairman on board was not aware of this little problem!

In around 1970 it was decided to greatly reduce the number of officers' saloons on the railway. In the past the general manager of the region, the civil engineer and others all had their own saloons for inspections. This was reduced to the general manager alone and the others were sold off. I was able to buy Great Eastern No. 1, which had a balcony on the rear where I could sit with a cigar and a glass of port if I so wished and see, hear and even smell the railway. It had a lounge with a wonderful leather button-backed seat, a lavatory, vestibule and kitchen, and the famous long table for fourteen people. It was fitted with a hatch to the kitchen and a bell to summon the steward. Of course, it also had heating, fans and a speedometer. Later, I was able to acquire a vehicle from the royal train, which had four bedrooms, two full baths, a lounge and an attendant's compartment. Taking a bath on the move was an interesting undertaking!

I was allowed to attach this mobile home on to West Highland service trains in the autumn when the trains were lightened. What a remarkable privilege this was. The only drawback was that the balcony could only trail one way, the other way being right behind the locomotive. An exhilarating experience, but rather a lot of exhaust!

I remember one day leaving Mallaig attached to the 06.30 service train and sitting on the balcony with the then Scottish Region general manager, the late Leslie Soane. As we passed a small footbridge, a majestic stag was standing on it with mist wreathing through its antlers – a moment never to be forgotten. On another occasion we set off on a trip to Oban. We got as far as Helensburgh at the start of the West Highland line and the locomotive failed. Another was fetched from Glasgow, but it too only achieved a short distance. I was approached by the guard, who told me that a lawyer had to get to court in Oban so they were laying on a bus and would I like to go. Thank you, but *no*! I had my day saloon full of food and drink and my night saloon, and we were parked with one of the finest views over the beautiful Clyde. Why would I want to take a *bus*?

Subsequently I had a marvellous week in Norfolk, travelling all the lines out of Norwich. I had requested this and was asked if £1,500 would be too much. I suppose this was a marginal costing; after all, the locomotive crew and guard were already employed. Another tour was over the branch lines of Cornwall, spending some nights in Penzance station. We were shown this territory by the redoubtable Rusty Eplett, who seemed to know everyone, but there was one moment as we went on to a branch when the guard said, 'Have you got the token, sir?'

'No, haven't you?' A hasty reversal was made and we set off again. What would have happened today? But the rulebook was normally slavishly followed.

We used GE1 for the Railway Heritage Trust. It was a great help in persuading councillors and representatives of other bodies to make a contribution to the cost of the refurbishment under review. We inspected Hull station and I requested the saloon be turned so that the balcony was on the rear going north. On the return from our meeting and lunch – no saloon! After enquiring we discovered the signalman would not let the saloon propel because it had been registered as a private charter instead of an officers' special. After some high-level discussion we were able to go on our way.

A similar thing happened when inspecting the Gunnislake branch. Unless we were allowed out with the saloon leading, we would have been there forever as there was no other way out. Layers of more and more senior management eventually unlocked the problem, but someone remarked to me that we should have some sympathy for the signalman, because if anything did go wrong, he would get the blame.

What a privilege it was for me to have my own train on the main line and I certainly made good use of it. I travelled from Penzance to Wick and Thurso via Georgemass Junction, plus the whole of Scotland, most of Wales, all the principal English lines, but only a bit of Southern. On one occasion on the Far North line we waved to people on a platform as we always did and they waved back. The guard at the other end of the saloon saw this, applied the brake and backed up the train, to be greeted by a rather embarrassed family who did not want to travel. 'In London, if you wave to a bus, it doesn't stop; in the Highlands the train not only stops but backs up to collect you,' said the man. Another time, via Bernard Kaukas, I invited John Betjeman on a trip around East London; clearly enjoying the vantage point afforded by the elevated lines, he said, 'From above is the finest way to see the churches of London.'

My saloon trips were greatly facilitated by Graeme Brocken, who was the volunteer steward and cook on board. Graeme worked in the timetable office at Crewe. I told him where I would like to go; he worked out what was possible and then submitted it. It was a sensible arrangement all round. One evening at Ipswich, where we were due to spend the night, we were asked to get off as no passengers were allowed on the movement to the sidings where we were to sleep overnight. Graeme protested that he was in the middle of cooking our evening meal and it would spoil if he got off. It was only when I pointed out that he was a fully paid up railwayman that he was allowed to stay.

I was introduced to saloon riding by the late Bill Thorpe, then general manager in Scotland, who invited me to travel on his saloon from Glasgow to Mallaig because my family had built the Fort William to Mallaig extension, including the Glenfinnan Viaduct. I regarded the invitation as a rare treat and I was hooked after that. On that first trip, Bill told me to wave to the permanent way men. I protested that I didn't work for the railway. 'They don't know that,' he replied, and so from then on I waved.

Another great railwayman was Bob Lawrence. I rode in his saloon, when he was general manager for London Midland Region, at 115mph according to his speedometer. It was quite impressive.

Now saloon GE1 and the sleeper are at my home and only move a few yards. GE1 has a wooden body and a wooden frame so I wouldn't insult the inspectors by asking to take it on the main line, but it went very well on its Gresley bogies at 100mph!

I have many happy memories of my salooning days. They gave me much pleasure and I am extremely grateful to all those who made them possible.

Glossary

ASLEF	Associated Society of Locomotive Engineers and Firemen
ASM	Assistant Station Manager
BRB	British Railways Board
DCC	Deputy Chief Controller
DM	District or Divisional Manager
DOS	District Operating Superintendent
DMU	Diesel Multiple Unit
ECML	East Coast Main Line
EMU	Electric Multiple Unit
FO	First-class open coach
GC	Great Central Railway
GE1	Great Eastern No. 1
GER	Great Eastern Railway
GN&GE	Great Northern & Great Eastern Railway
GN&LNW	Great Northern & London & North Western Railway
GNR	Great Northern Railway
GUV	General Utility Van (for parcels traffic)
GWR	Great Western Railway
LDC	Local Departmental Committee (for negotiation and consultation)
LDEC	Lancashire, Derbyshire & East Coast Railway
LMS	London, Midland & Scottish Railway
LNER	London & North Eastern Railway
LT&S	London, Tilbury & Southend Railway
M&GN	Midland & Great Northern Railway
MoD	Ministry of Defence
PWI	Permanent Way Inspector
TSSA	Transport Salaried Staff Association
TUC	Trades Union Congress

BD container	A common type of box container for carrying freight requiring road collection or delivery. Carried on Conflat wagons.
Bolster wagon	A long, low, flat wagon with bogie wheels and stanchions.
Buckeye	A secure automatic coach coupling.
Cess	The space alongside the track.
Demurrage	A charge for detaining wagons beyond the free period.
Distant	The caution signal preceding Home and Starter stop signals.
Grove	The code name for a royal train.
Light engine	A locomotive running without vehicles.
Mogul	A locomotive with 2-6-0 wheel arrangement; Pacific 4-6-2.

Off the road   Colloquial term for a derailment.

Parly   Derived from Parliamentary Trains, and an 1844 Act requiring one train to run daily over all routes and serving all stations.

Possession   An engineer's line blockage.

Privs   Concessionary reduced price tickets for staff.

Six-foot   A colloquial term for the distance between the tracks.

Top Link   The highest train crew group.

RUNNING a railway is a complex business. However organised it is, there will always be surprises: often hilarious, frequently unexpected, but sometimes serious. *Along Different Lines* includes such bizarre 'everyday' events as coping with hurricanes, rogue locomotives and runaway wagons, PR successes and otherwise, the Brighton Belle, *Flying Scotsman* and *Mallard*, training course capers, a wino invasion, trackside antics, the Eurostar backdrop, the birth of a prison, and royal and other special occasions. Expert authors Geoff Body and Bill Parker have lovingly put together this entertaining collection in which railway professionals recall notable incidents from across their careers. This illustrated compilation provides an enjoyable look back at life on the railways.

GEOFF BODY worked in the railway industry from 1945 to 1976 and has been writing on railways and other subjects ever since. Bill Parker's thirty-nine-year railway career began at Doncaster in 1945 and progressed through to Divisional Manager at King's Cross. Together they have written the popular *Signal Box Coming Up, Sir!* for The History Press.

£9.99
ISBN 978-0-7524-8915-5

9 780752 489155

www.thehistorypress.co.uk

SAINT THÉRÈSE OF LISIEUX
and her Sisters

JENNIFER MOORCROFT

SAINT THÉRÈSE OF LISIEUX AND HER SISTERS